Praise for *The Forever Letter*

"*The Forever Letter* is an exceptional book. Rabbi Zaiman offers moving stories and profound insights that have the potential to enrich, even transform, your most important relationships. It's a book to read and give to members of your family."—Michael Josephson, founder of the Josephson Institute of Ethics and CHARACTER COUNTS!

"When I finished reading *The Forever Letter* I was so inspired, I sat down to write a forever letter to my children."   —Rabbi Sherre Hirsch, author of *Thresholds: How to Thrive Through Life's Transitions to Live Fearlessly and Regret-Free*

"*The Forever Letter* is one of those rare books that could change your life. It is chock full of stories—from the author's own life and from the lives of hundreds of people she's worked with—that will inspire readers of all ages to reflect on what and who is important to them and to express these values and this bond in a letter to a loved one. The author's gorgeous writing is mesmerizing and intimate and insightful and will get you writing even if you are no writer. Highly recommended."   —Priscilla Long, author of *Fire and Stone: Where Do We Come From? What Are We? Where Are We Going?*

"In her beautiful book, *The Forever Letter*, Elana breathes critical life back into the healing art of letters. With joy and insight, she shows us how to use the written word to heal our relationships and live with greater intention. It is the perfect gift for our hectic and frenzied hearts."—Rev. Susan Sparks, author of *Laugh Your Way to Grace*

"Here is a book to help you clarify your deepest values, and transmit them. Rabbi Zaiman shows us how to leave not a legacy of possessions, but the legacy of a life."—Rabbi David Wolpe, author of *David: The Divided Harp*

"One of the most important ways to support wise aging."—Rabbi Rachel Cowan, co-author of *Wise Aging: Living with Joy, Resilience, & Spirit*

"*The Forever Letter* is an invaluable resource for anyone involved in the estate planning area. I plan to recommend Elana's book to my clients as a matter of course. If more people composed thoughtful forever letters in conjunction with their estate plans, I believe many painful will and trust disputes could be avoided."—William L. Fleming, estate planning counsel

"Step by step, Elana guides us to bring the essence of who we are to the page."   —Rabbi Angela Buchdahl, Central Synagogue Manhattan

"Rabbi Zaiman showed me that forever letters are one of the most important gifts we can give to people we love and care about. Leaving words from our heart is just as important as passing on our material possessions. I will be recommending this book to clients and friends."—Barbara A. Isenhour, elder law and estate planning attorney, Somers Tamblyn King Isenhour Bleck

"The starting place for developing and implementing a successful family financial, wealth management, or philanthropy plan is understanding our clients' core values. Elana Zaiman's book *The Forever Letter* is a valuable addition to the advisor's toolkit for helping families clarify and prioritize their core values."   —John Goodwin, founder of Filament, LLC

"I found Elana's approach to sharing our values thought-provoking. It made me realize we do not share enough meaningful and heartfelt words with the people we love during life. Using her approach, we can keep clients centered on their values, on what they want their family to remember in the present and long after they are gone, especially if something happens unexpectedly and they are no longer able to communicate what is in their soul. A great gift for you and for your clients."—Carolyn McClanahan, MD, CFP®, Life Planning Partners, Inc

the
FOREVER
LETTER

Photo by Autumn Azure

ABOUT THE AUTHOR

Elana Zaiman (Seattle, WA) serves as the chaplain for elders at The Summit at First Hill in Seattle. She also serves as an adjunct faculty member with the Harborview Clinical Pastoral Education (CPE) program at Harborview Medical Center and as a motivational speaker and scholar-in-residence on topics such as forgiveness, healing, vulnerability, and compassion. She is a columnist for *Liv Fun*, a magazine created for Leisure Care, and her writing has been featured in other magazines, literary journals, anthologies, and newspapers. Visit her online at www.ElanaZaiman.com.

TO WRITE THE AUTHOR

If you wish to contact the author or would like more information about this book, please write to the author in care of Llewellyn Worldwide, and we will forward your request. We cannot guarantee that every letter written to the author can be answered, but all will be forwarded. Please write to:

Elana Zaiman
℅ Llewellyn Worldwide
2143 Wooddale Drive
Woodbury, MN 55125-2989

Please enclose a self-addressed stamped envelope for reply,
or $1.00 to cover costs. If outside the USA, enclose
an international postal reply coupon.

Many of Llewellyn's authors have websites with additional information and resources. For more information, please visit www.llewellyn.com.

the FOREVER LETTER

Writing What We Believe for Those We Love

Elana Zaiman

Llewellyn Publications
Woodbury, Minnesota

FIRST EDITION
Third Printing, 2018

Book design by Bob Gaul
Cover design by Ellen Lawson
Editing by Laura Graves

Llewellyn Publications is a registered trademark of Llewellyn Worldwide Ltd.

Library of Congress Cataloging-in-Publication Data
  Names: Zaiman, Elana, 1962– author.
   Title: The forever letter: writing what we believe for those we love / Elana
    Zaiman.
   Description: First Edition. | Woodbury: Llewellyn Worldwide, Ltd., 2017. |
    Includes bibliographical references.
   Identifiers: LCCN 2017029246 (print) | LCCN 2017021581 (ebook) | ISBN
    9780738753720 (ebook) | ISBN 9780738752884
   Subjects: LCSH: Wills, Ethical—History and criticism. | Wills,
    Ethical—Authorship. | Letters of last instructions. | Last letters before
    death. | Conduct of life.
   Classification: LCC BJ1286.W6 (print) | LCC BJ1286.W6 Z89 2017 (ebook) | DDC
    170/.44—dc23
   LC record available at https://lccn.loc.gov/2017029246

Llewellyn Publications
A Division of Llewellyn Worldwide Ltd.
2143 Wooddale Drive
Woodbury, MN 55125-2989
www.llewellyn.com

Printed in the United States of America

CONTENTS

COPYRIGHT LISTING

A NOTE TO READERS

Many of the names, identities, places, and time frames in this book have been changed to protect people's privacy. On occasion I have created one person to stand for a composite of people, and I have altered the facts of a few stories while remaining true to their essence.

In honor of my mother, Ann, and my father, Joel
My teachers from the beginning
My teachers to this day
and
In memory of their son, my brother, Rafael Moshe.

INTRODUCTION

What a lot we lost when we stopped writing letters.
You can't reread a phone call.
—LIZ CARPENTER[1]

THE POWER OF LETTERS

Years ago, we wrote letters to communicate with one another. These days, we text, instant message, and tweet. We tend to think of letter writing as old-fashioned and unnecessary—a craft of bygone days, a relic of ancient times—much like a horse-drawn carriage, an icebox, or an oil lamp, but letter writing need not be relegated to the past.

Born in the early sixties, I grew up in what was still a letter-writing generation. To this day, I keep a box of letters I've saved over the years: letters from summer camp, Junior Year Abroad, and from my professional

---

1   Liz Carpenter, *Getting Better All the Time* (College Station, TX: Texas A&M University Press, 1993), 263.

years as a rabbi and a chaplain. Letters from my parents, grandparents, brothers and sister, aunts and uncles, cousins, friends, boyfriends, teachers, mentors, students, nieces. Letters from my husband, Seth, and my son, Gabriel. I also keep a three-ring binder of loving e-mail letters from family and friends that I've printed out over the past decade for fear they would get lost in the virtual world or deleted because of a computer crash.

On days when I feel out of sorts, I return to these letters. They strengthen me when I don't believe in myself, remind me who I am when I question my purpose or my values, and enable me to better reflect on my relationships and on my life. As I reread these letters, I experience a sense of gratitude for the love, concern, appreciation, compassion, kindness, wisdom, guidance, and honesty that many of these letters impart. I also experience a sense of gratitude toward the people who took the time to write them.

This book is about writing a certain kind of letter that I'm calling the *forever letter*. The forever letter is simply this: a heartfelt letter that we write to the people who are most important to us with the hope that, even if the letter itself isn't kept forever, the wisdom and love that we share will be.

None of us come to writing a forever letter from the same place. We enter from wherever we are. We can write forever letters when we or the person(s) we're writing to reach milestones or critical junctures in life. Milestones such as becoming a parent, grandparent, aunt, or uncle; reaching a special birthday; coming of age; graduating; entering college; falling in love; marrying; giving birth; receiving a job offer; retiring. Critical junctures such as being expelled from school; getting laid off; divorcing; receiving a life-threatening diagnosis; living through the death of a loved one; or when we, ourselves, are dying. But we don't have to wait. We can write forever letters at any time.

HISTORICAL INSPIRATION

The forever letter is inspired by the medieval Jewish tradition of the *ethical will*, a letter parents would write to their children, stating their prescriptions for living meaningful Jewish lives by following certain ethical and ritual precepts.[2] Yes, ethical values had been imparted in biblical and rabbinic literature for centuries, but unique to medieval times was the emergence of an ethical literature that encompassed ethical treatises, homiletic works, and ethical wills. The treatises and homiletic works were written by scholars, but the ethical will—more practical, autobiographical, and personal in nature— was a venue open to nonscholars as well.[3]

When did these parents write their ethical wills? Some wrote when they felt they were nearing the end of their lives. Others wrote in their earlier years and revised their letters over time, and there were those who wrote when they traveled or were separated from their families for extended periods of time, and feared for their safe return. These letters shared a sense of urgency—the need to get words down in writing just in case this was the only opportunity.

The style of these early letters varied from objective and reserved to more personal and reflective, from a commanding (at times even admonishing) tone to a more gentle tone, and in the amount of space devoted to ritual versus ethical precepts. Many authors asked for or offered God's blessings. Some told stories, shared personal experiences, or provided historical information. Some asked for or offered forgiveness. Some stated their ultimate truth. Many requested their words to be read often: daily, weekly, monthly, or yearly. For those interested in delving into these texts a little more deeply, see appendix A.

It is to the forever letter that I bring these elements of the ethical will: a desire to communicate what we believe to those we love; a sense of urgency

---

2 Israel Abrahams, *Hebrew Ethical Wills* (Philadelphia: The Jewish Publication Society, 2006), 7. It is believed that the term *ethical will* originated with Israel Abrahams, who in 1926 compiled a scholarly study of these letters. In Hebrew, they are called *tze-vah-oat*, "commandments."

3 Joseph Dan, *Encyclopaedia Judaica*, v. 16, s.v. "ethical wills." Jerusalem, Israel: Keter Publishing House, 1972.

to put our words on paper because we don't know how much time we have; a chance to share our personal experiences, histories, and stories, to highlight our values, to forgive and to ask for forgiveness, to state hard truths, to state our ultimate truth, to offer blessings; and a hope that our words will be read for years to come.

I began teaching on the topic of ethical wills when I was ordained as a rabbi in 1993, but it wasn't until the early 2000s that I began to take my teaching on the road. When I did, I met people at airports and train stations, on airplanes and trains, who would ask me where I was going. I'd respond, "I'm going to a community to teach on the topic of ethical wills."

Most people had no idea what ethical wills were. Some thought the term *ethical will* referred to writing a last will and testament in an ethical manner. Others thought it referred to writing a health-care directive or a living will. I explained that it was neither, that an ethical will was a letter we wrote to our children or our grandchildren to pass on our values. People resonated with the idea immediately, but the unanimous response went something like this: If you want to encourage people to write this letter, you can't call it an ethical will. It's not sexy enough.

There was another reason I couldn't call this letter an ethical will. Ethical wills are about imparting values from the older to the younger generation, and I had an experience early on in my teaching that enabled me to see this approach was too limited. I returned to Park Avenue Synagogue, the community where I began my rabbinic career, to serve as a scholar-in-residence on the topic of ethical wills. At the time, Amy, a congregant and friend, told me that her son, Will (by then a college graduate), worked in town, wanted to see me, and planned to come to the evening writing workshop. She had suggested to him that this might be the wrong venue since he had no children or grandchildren to write to, but Will said this was the only free time he had in his schedule, so he'd be there. I was honored he was making time to see me. I had watched Will grow from a preteen to a young adult. The last time I had seen him, he'd been in his sophomore year of high school.

On the evening of the workshop, Will appeared. He was a taller, more handsome version of himself, still slender, light-skinned, wide-eyed with thick brown hair, and the same smile, gusto, and enthusiasm. Aside from Will and a single woman on staff, the group that evening consisted of parents and grandparents. Before I presented the writing prompts, I gave Will the option of writing a letter to himself looking ahead five years into his future and contemplating the values he hoped to carry forward or of writing a letter to his parents to thank them for all he had learned in their home. I told him he could either write to the prompts or just do his own thing. Will wrote along with the group. I had no idea which option he had chosen until the next day, when I saw his mother.

Amy came up to me and said, "Last night I received the most beautiful letter I've ever received." I later learned that Will had used the prompts I had presented to the group that evening to write to his parents.

For me, what began as an exercise to welcome Will into the community of ethical will writers who were passing their values forward turned into seeing the ethical will as inspiration for a new kind of letter, the forever letter, a letter that would enable preteens, teens, and young adults to express their values, love, and appreciation (to ask for forgiveness and to forgive) backward; adults in their fifties, sixties, and seventies, still blessed with parents, aunts, uncles, teachers, and mentors to do the same; and people who may not have elders or children in their lives, but who certainly have values, love, and appreciation to share, as well as forgiveness they want to ask for or grant, to write to their spouses, siblings, and friends.

While it's true that writing letters to our children or grandchildren to pass on our values is a profoundly different experience from writing letters to our parents, grandparents, teachers, partners, spouses, or friends, there's a common thread that all these letters share, and it is this: the desire to live our values with greater intention, to better understand ourselves, to make ourselves known to the people we love, and to heal what may be broken between us.

THIS BOOK AND ITS INTENT

The Forever Letter begins with the story of receiving my father's ethical will, and describes what it meant to me when I received it, how it has continued to be a source of strength to me over the years, and how it served as the foundation for me on my journey toward developing the forever letter.

To make writing forever letters part of your life plan, you have to know why doing so is crucial. In chapter 2, I inspire you to write by exploring potential benefits. Inspirations include recognizing that sometimes we can write what we cannot speak; we can come to better understand ourselves and our relationships; we can make ourselves known; we can ask for forgiveness and we can forgive; we can clarify our values and live with greater intention.

You may be one who will immediately take to writing forever letters or you may be one who will resist, who will say, "I'm not a writer," or "I'm afraid I'll say something damaging," or "I don't want to think about death. I'm still young. I have plenty of time." Chapter 3 presents these and other reasons you might resist and motivates you to let go of your resistance and to write.

Chapter 4 encourages you to contemplate what matters to you most. I explore in detail eleven topics—among them live your truth, give, love, never stop asking questions.

Chapters 5 and 6 are the heart of this book. They ask you to consider the frame of mind and heart you bring to the page. Chapter 5 suggests ways to approach your writing to increase your chances of being heard, such as be present, share personal experiences, and be vulnerable. Chapter 6 suggests things to avoid—among them favoritism, telling family secrets, lying to others and to ourselves.

From inspiration to motivation and contemplation, I move to action—writing. Chapter 7 offers thoughts on the writing process, such as finding a comfortable place to write and being open to emotions. Chapter 8 presents writing prompts—sentence completions, questions, and techniques for stirring it up—all designed to help you access your deepest emotions and express your innermost self. Chapter 9 offers guidance on writing and editing your forever letter so you can feel pleased with your creation.

You'll find additional information in the appendices. Appendix A has excerpts from ethical wills of old. Appendix B has excerpts from the first forever letter I wrote to my son, as well as my thoughts on the process of writing this letter to him. Appendix C has the sentence completion prompts and the question prompts from chapter 8 to give you easy access when you begin to generate material for your forever letter.

In this age of instant and constant communication, many consider writing letters to be anachronistic. *The Forever Letter* debunks that belief, proving instead that forever letters are perfect containers for our most precious nonmaterial possessions—our beliefs, wisdom, love, appreciation, forgiveness, and more—and showing how, like any material object we craft or build, the process enriches, grows, and helps us push ourselves to become our best.

Over the years, I've had the opportunity to refine my teaching; to learn from family, friends, neighbors, cab drivers, fellow travelers, and from those who've come to study with me and in turn have become my teachers. Based on their comments, feedback, suggestions, stories, and questions, I've deepened my approach. This book is the result.

I believe we should all write forever letters. That is why I teach and speak and write about them. That is why I wrote this book: to persuade you to write forever letters to the people you love and to guide you along in the process.

An Invitation

May we learn to open in love
so all the doors and windows
of our bodies swing wide
on their rusty hinges.

May we learn to give ourselves with both hands,
to lift each other on our shoulders,
to carry one another along.

May holiness move in us
so we pay attention to its small voice
and honor its light in each other. [4]

—Dawna Markova

---

4   Dawna Markova, "May we learn to open in love…" in *Prayers for Healing: 365
Blessings, Poems, & Meditations from Around the World*, ed. Maggie Oman Shannon
(Boston, MA: Conari Press, 2000), 41.

1

MY FATHER'S FOREVER
LETTER TO HIS
CHILDREN

Respect one another, even if love is not always possible.
—JOEL ZAIMAN

It happened when I was fourteen. My father, the rabbi of Temple Emanu-El in Providence, Rhode Island, came home after work one day, handed me a booklet, and said, "Here! One of these is mine."

I stared at the mimeographed, staple-stitched, off-white card-stock booklet. The cover, penned in black ink, featured a scroll hanging from a filigreed signpost. Calligraphed inside the scroll, the title: *A Collection of Ethical Wills.* I had no idea what ethical wills were, why my father had written one, or why he wanted me to read it; but I did know that I loved listening to my father's sermons so I was intrigued. My father, a passionate orator and a beloved spiritual leader who was a giant not only to me but to our entire community, had never before handed me something he had written. What was it that he had written and wanted so much for me to read?

I flipped through the booklet. I noticed letters addressed to children by their parents. The letters began in any number of ways: "My beloved children," "To my children," "My dearest daughter," "To my sons." Sometimes the letters closed with "Love." Other times, with the words, "Your loving Mother" or "Love, Dad."

"So, which one is yours?" I asked.

My father wouldn't tell me. It became a game. If I wanted to guess, I could guess, and he would tell me whether or not I was right. I was now even more intrigued. My father was not usually so playful.

I retreated into our wood-paneled den, sat down on our white leather couch, opened the booklet, and read the introduction that my father had authored. I learned that ethical wills were letters that passed on values from one generation to the next. I learned that my father had just finished teaching an adult education class in our synagogue on ethical wills, and that after studying these ancient texts with his class he had given them the assignment to write an ethical will. I also learned that this booklet was the result.

In search of his letter, I skimmed through this booklet as if I were Sherlock Holmes seeking to solve the latest mystery. I eliminated the letters addressed only to daughters and only to sons. I eliminated the letters signed by mothers. I focused instead on the letters addressed to multiple children and on those that closed with the words, "Love, Dad" or "Love." Of these, I read only the first two or three sentences. That was all I needed to read to determine whether a letter needed to remain in the mix.

In this manner, I made my way through this booklet of eighteen letters, making asterisks next to the four I thought could be my father's. My goal was not to make the winning guess. My goal was to make my way through this booklet as quickly as possible, to return to my father with my asterisks, to receive confirmation of one of my choices, and to spend time reading his letter.

Within minutes I handed my father the booklet with my four asterisks, and he confirmed one of my choices. I walked back into the den, sat
on the couch, and began to read. I had to be alone. Here are his words:

To my children,

I expect you to take care of your mother—wherever she may
be...whatever she chooses to do. You honor me by honoring her.
More important—you honor yourselves, for she gave you life.

Respect one another, even if love is not always possible. Take
care of each other...always. Your loyalty to each other was one
of the chief joys of my life.

We have often disagreed. As you grew older, we differed
concerning substantive matters, and I was proud of how you all
stood your ground, even when I attempted to intimidate. You all
thought clearly and argued well. Nor were any of you lacking in
a sense of humor.

There were times when each of you thought I was unfair—
that I was picking on you. Sometimes you were right. Think
about it, however, and you will realize that I picked on you when
you most behaved like me...at least like those aspects of myself
that I liked least...my own weaknesses, if you will. I am glad
you survived my unfairness with your integrity intact and the
deep realization of how much I loved you all.

I hope you have learned, too, to recognize your own
weaknesses...primarily so that they can become your strengths.
So often, what we think of as weaknesses and strengths are
culturally determined. You are what you are—and I hope and pray
each of you realizes how good and how wonderful you are. Part of
your goodness is some of those things you think of as weaknesses.
Without them, however, you would not be you. So, do not be
ashamed of them. Be proud. They are really your strengths.

I know you will remain proud Jews as long as you remain proud of your own selves. I expect you all to continue to grow as Jews—to learn and to teach, to fulfill and to obey.

Your mother and I tried hard to teach you that we were different ... that you are different ... as Jews, and therefore, as people. You learned, too, that difference has its price. I hope you are convinced, as we are convinced, that being a Jew is well worth that price; and when you feel, as you will sometimes, that it is not, that you realize that you are you, and you have no alternative.

In the process of growing, and sometimes even as grown-ups, to "be different" was not enough of an explanation of how things really were. You wanted to know: Are we better or worse? When asked, Mother and I answered: We think we are better. For us to have said: It's all the same, would have been to lie.

Yet, I hope you understand that "better" is more a description of context than of kind. We have tried to teach you by example that the difference between good and bad is primarily the situations in which you allow yourself to be found. You never know what you would have done had you been in the other fellow's shoes. It is up to you (and this is where you exercise complete control—do not allow yourself the luxury of any excuses!) to stay in your own shoes, and let them always be on firm ground.

Say *Kaddish* [the memorial prayer] after me when I die ... for me ... for you ... for Israel ... for God ... for you.

I have always thanked God for you. May He continue to watch over you ... always ... and always.

Love, [5]

---

5   My father uses a series of periods as a style feature. The "dots" are his as he wrote the letter, not ellipses denoting that any part of his letter has been deleted. Translation inserted in brackets.

I read my father's letter over and over. His words coursed through my veins as if I were receiving a blood transfusion. Each time I read it, I cried. There was no doubt in my mind that, had I taken the time to read through all four letters I had asterisked, I would have chosen this one. As I read my father's words, I heard his voice, his inflections and intonations, his pauses and his silences as clearly as if he were standing next to me and speaking into my ear.

I loved and respected my father very much, and, after reading his letter, I came to love and respect him even more. Here was my father expressing his values, wisdom, and love to us, his children: Elana, fourteen; Sarina, eleven; Ari, ten; and Rafi, nine. Here was my father speaking from his heart, saying what he wanted and needed to say, being vulnerable— more vulnerable than I had ever known him to be. Here was my father admitting his weaknesses. Here was my father being human.

My father never feigned perfection, but it appeared to me that at least in the eyes of the community, he was as close to perfect as one could get. As a beloved rabbi and community leader, rarely a day passed without someone telling me how amazing my father was. They'd say things like, "Your father gave an amazing sermon on Friday night," or "It was so thoughtful of your father to visit my husband in the hospital," or "Your father gives great advice," or "Your father is a gifted teacher," or "Your father delivered a wonderful eulogy at my mother's funeral."

I was always proud of my father, yet as an adolescent, and a rather innocent one, these words of constant praise sometimes bothered me. I didn't understand that my father could be so highly regarded by a community and still be imperfect. As I look back, I'm not sure the community did either. From the 1960s (even prior) until the 1980s (perhaps even to this day), many communities seemed to invest their clergy with an otherworldly holiness that exempted their clergy from being human. I remember friends asking me questions like, "Does your father take out the garbage? Does he swear?" Reading my father's letter was a revelation of sorts. It showed me that even though the community held him in such high regard, he knew he wasn't perfect; he knew he was human. This gave me permission to see him as imperfect and human, too.

Let me be clear. Had my father never written us this letter, I would have known who he was. I would have known what he stood for. I would have known what he considered important, but I'm not sure I would have highlighted the points he chose to highlight, nor would I have known how he understood himself, his strengths and his weaknesses, his virtues and his shortcomings; and, while I may have been able to guess his expectations for us, I'm certain I would not have articulated them the way he did.

I imagine it wasn't easy for my father to confront himself, but I sense he understood that to impart what mattered to him most, he had to put himself on the page. I sense he knew that there was no escaping the page, that on the page his words sat in bold relief and could be returned to and read over and over again.

My father handed me his letter in 1976. When I received it, I knew I would hold onto it forever. To this day, I continue to read it. Yes, my father's still alive. We communicate by e-mail. We talk on the phone, though our day-to-day e-mails and phone calls don't carry the same depth of emotion. They aren't meant to. Besides, my father hates the phone. His usual greeting when any of his children call is, "Hi, I'll get your mother." If he stays on the phone for more than a few minutes, we assume it's because our mother's not home.

So, when I want to hear my father's voice in a deep and personal way, or when I want to feel closer to him, I read this letter. It connects me to him when I need that connection, when I'm angry with him, in awe of him, feeling lost, or when I miss him because he lives in Baltimore and I live in Seattle. As I age, reading this letter helps me better understand my father, myself, and our relationship. It also takes me back to a time in our family when we were four children, before my youngest brother, Rafi, was diagnosed with Ewing's sarcoma and died at the age of eleven. My father's words serve as a memorial to my family of origin, once six, now five.

Sometimes, I find myself wondering how different my father's words would have been had he written to us a few months after Rafi died. Would he have reflected more on his faith, fears, disappointments, or regrets? Other times, I find myself wondering what my father, now in his late seventies, would write to each of his three living children, now adults and parents with children of our own.

Over the years, I've asked him to write us another letter to fill in the gap of the last forty years and to further enhance my understanding of him and myself. I've told him that I long to set his first letter alongside a second, to hear his voice as a father of young children alongside his voice as a father of adult children, the parents of his grandchildren. Each time I ask, he looks at me with questioning eyes, as if to say: Isn't one enough?

I must adopt a new strategy. Next time I'll ask him to consider writing a letter to his eight grandchildren so that they, too, will have words to which they can return, to hear their grandfather's voice, to feel their grandfather's presence, and to be the recipients of their grandfather's guidance and love.

2

WHY WRITE A FOREVER LETTER?

Life is a journey in self-discovery. If we're not growing, we're not living fully. Growth requires self-examination.
—SUSAN L. TAYLOR[6]

Many of us—parents, children, grandparents, grandchildren, aunts, uncles, nieces, nephews, teachers, students, siblings, spouses, partners, and friends—entertain the idea of writing a forever letter, but we're on the fence, we're not sure it matters. In the following pages, I hope to inspire you to write by exploring the potential benefits.

---

6   Susan L. Taylor, "In The Spirit," in *Essence*, October 1992, 55.

It's a Tangible, Lasting Gift

I often ask people if they've received any meaningful letters over the years, and if they have, what those letters have meant to them. Here are some of their responses:

Jerry, in his sixties, said: "After hearing your talk last night, I went home, searched through my scrapbooks, and discovered a letter my mother had written to me when I was thirteen and away at summer camp. The letter read, 'Dear Jerry, be strong and of good courage. I miss you.'" Jerry's voice filled with tears as he spoke his mother's words. He said that, until he found this letter, all he could remember about his mother was her complaining and her depression, but that rereading her letter reminded him of her love and hopes for him. He said that he had been wanting to write a letter to his children for some time but couldn't seem to motivate himself to write it, until now. Somehow after reading his mother's letter, he felt ready.

Howard, in his late forties, talked about his sister who died at forty-five, having struggled with breast cancer for many years. He said that before she died she wrote a letter to each of her siblings. He cherishes his letter.

Roxanne, twenty-five, mentioned an emotional three-page letter she had received from her father when she was nine and her father was in divinity school. She talked about hanging that letter on a nail in her bedroom, where it remained until the first page, then the second page, and finally the last page got lost. Though she no longer has that letter, she continues to carry its contents in her heart.

Olivia said that every year on their birthdays her parents wrote her and her siblings long thoughtful letters. They got presents, too, but her parents made it clear that the letter was more important. Writing these letters was her parents' expectation of themselves, but it was also their expectation of their children, who were all expected to write birthday letters to each other, and to their parents too. They started when they were young by drawing pictures, but as they got older, their parents encouraged them to write meaningful letters. Olivia said that she still has those letters and that they continue to write them.

Victoria, in her mid-sixties, told a story about her husband, Scott. Scott hadn't grown up with his dad. His parents had divorced when he was young, but when Scott was in the army and stationed near his dad, he reached out to his father to reconnect. At that time, Scott was in his forties and his father was in his sixties, and they were lucky to have had a ten-year relationship before his father died. Scott was fifty when his father scribbled this note to him:

Scott,

I can't believe you are 50 (on June 22nd).

I'm too young to have a 50-year-old son—but most important, I have a son I'm most proud of.

With all my love,
Dad & Margaret

P.S. Stay healthy and have many more happy birthdays.

Victoria said that this was the only note Scott ever received from his father, and that when she found it in his wallet many years later, she framed it and put it on his bedside table so that he could see it every day. It brought him comfort.

Jackie talked about a letter she received back in the 1980s from a friend of hers who had AIDS telling her how much he appreciated having her in his life. She hadn't known her friend had AIDS when she received his letter. It was taboo back then to talk about it. She spoke about how much his letter meant to her.

Viv shared with me a letter that she had received from her thirty-five-year-old daughter, Audrey, who became a hemiplegic at the age of twenty-five. Audrey wrote this letter to her mom as she watched her mom care for her mother, Esther (Audrey's grandmother), who was in her mid-eighties and living with Parkinson's and Alzheimer's.

Dearest Mom,

I have noticed how lovingly and thoroughly you have been caring for Mama Esther. It makes me feel terrible knowing that I won't be able to do the same for you when, heaven forbid, you're in the same position, needing help or transportation or any kind of help.

I'm sure Dad can always be there to help you with most of it, but what happens when it's my turn to step in because you just happen to need your daughter. How will I come to you when you need me?

I thought the only way and the best way is to give you this gift, and let you know that I wish I could be like you as a daughter. I just want you to know that with me, you've ALWAYS got a friend.

All my love always,

When Viv received this letter, she said it brought tears to her eyes.

Becky, fifty-one, was diagnosed with AVM, a congenital condition that causes bleeding in the brain. Two of Becky's symptoms are numbness and hearing loss. The good news: Becky can recover from these symptoms. The bad news: her diagnosis remains. Maybe her brain will bleed again, maybe it won't. Add to her diagnosis a small aneurysm her medical team discovered during her MRI. Add to that aneurysm the fact that both her mother and her father died young. The reason my friend Linda wrote to me about Becky was to tell me that, during the time of Becky's diagnosis, Becky discovered a bunch of letters that her parents had written to her when she was twenty and studying in England. These letters brought Becky joy. Though her parents were no longer alive, though they couldn't hug her or speak to her, they were still present through their words, and their words comforted.

I disagree with Feng Shui advisors who suggest destroying old letters (especially old love letters) because getting rid of the old makes way for the new. When we write letters to the people we love, we give them a tangible gift that they can embrace for life: a gift that they can touch and hold; a gift that reminds them of our love for them and our appreciation of them; a gift that becomes a permanent brick in the structure of our relationship and that strengthens our bond. Old letters document the transitions in our lives. Yes, we change throughout the course of our lives, but who we are at one particular moment in time is part of our story, and who the person we're writing to is at one particular moment in time is part of our story. When the people we love want access to us and to our relationship, they may want this part of our story.

What about you? Do you remember letters you've received over the years? Letters sent by post or by e-mail? Letters written to you when you were at summer camp, in the military, at college, or studying abroad? Letters written to you on your birthday, when you graduated high school, college, or graduate school? Letters written to you when you married, when you birthed or adopted your first child, when you miscarried, when someone in your family died, when you were laid off, divorced, diagnosed with breast cancer, prostate cancer, or AIDS? What about love letters? What about letters speaking to the awesome way you handled a particular situation, challenging you to be a better self, or asking you for forgiveness? What about letters you received just because?

If you've saved any of these letters, find them. Reread them. Let them remind you of the people you love(d) and the people who love(d) you. Let them remind you of your strengths, gifts, values, struggles, challenges, failures, and successes. Let them remind you who you were, who you are, who you can be. Let them inspire you to write to the people you love.

Lest you think your words don't matter:

In one workshop, Nick, in his fifties, spoke about how, in the process of caring for his elderly mother, he had to open her safe deposit box to access her financial papers. When he did, he discovered two sealed letters addressed to him. He was excited to read them, but couldn't because they were not yet his to read. So, he left them where he found them. A few years later, after his mother died, Nick returned to her safe deposit box, eager to read these letters, but they were gone. He was devastated. Even as he retold this story, he had a hard time holding back his tears.

In another workshop, after asking participants what motivated them to attend, Rhoda, in her late fifties, reported that she had talked to her son that morning, and told him she would be attending a writing workshop to write letters to her grandchildren. She said her son was silent for a few moments before he asked in a soft voice, "Mom, will you write one to me, too?"

Our words do matter. Especially to the people we love.

SOMETIMES WE CAN WRITE WHAT WE CANNOT SPEAK

Max was in his sixties when he told me about his father, who had not been verbally communicative but who had been self-aware enough to know this about himself. To compensate for his lack of verbal communication skills, he wrote Max letters. It was through these letters that Max and his father tended their relationship.

Cora, in her fifties, said that when she was a teenager, she and her father had trouble communicating. One day she had the idea of leaving him a letter in his suitcase when he traveled on business, which he did often. It worked. He appreciated her notes and would respond from wherever his travels took him. Their letter writing continued for years, and in their letters they worked out a lot of issues.

Danielle, also in her fifties, talked about her father, a judgmental man with a temper that worsened as he aged. She said that toward the end of his life he wrote a letter to his children in which he wrote things he had never been able to say in person. He wrote that he was sorry he had made mistakes, that he wasn't the best father he could have been, that he did the best he could. He took responsibility for his fatherhood.

The Human Comedy by William Saroyan is a coming-of-age novel set in Ithaca, California, during World War II. Homer Macauley, the main character, is a boy of fourteen who longs to become a telegraph operator. Homer's brother, Marcus, goes to fight in the war. Scared of not returning home, Marcus writes Homer a letter before heading off to the front. In this letter, Marcus passes on his possessions—his clothes, bicycle, phonograph, rock collection, fishing gear—but he also imparts his values, ideals, hopes, faith, and love. He writes about how much he misses Homer and how he hopes to see him soon. He shares his thoughts about the war, his fears about what lies ahead, and his hope to return to Ithaca, to his girlfriend, and to create a family of his own. He also officially appoints Homer as the new head of the family and expresses his belief in Homer to both carry the family forward and keep the family together. The final paragraph of Marcus's letter begins with the words, "I can say in a letter what I could never say in speech."[7]

Marcus is not alone. Sometimes it's easier for us to express our emotions in writing than it is for us to express them verbally. Today, we are witnessing a communication revolution. Our teens are out there texting away. We say this is their downfall; always on their screens, they don't know how to talk to each other in person about stuff that matters. Perhaps that's true, but maybe, just maybe, we communicate more honestly and truthfully by texting and e-mailing than we do face-to-face, as recent research from the University of Nebraska reports.[8]

---

7 William Saroyan, *The Human Comedy* (New York: Dell Pub., 1971), 166–168.

8 Jordan Valinsky, "Study: It's Easier to Tell the Truth Over Text So Why Bother Speaking Anymore?" *Yahoo! news*, December 23, 2013, www.yahoo.com/news /study-easier-tell-truth-over-text-why-bother-145506847.html.

A divorced friend of mine, who spent months on the online dating scene, told me that she couldn't believe how much she had revealed in the long e-mails she had written to men she hardly knew. She believed the anonymity of the screen enabled her to feel more comfortable, safe, open, and uninhibited than she would have felt in person.

Some of us have trouble speaking to the people we love about the things that are most important to us. Perhaps it's easier for us to write down our words. Writing a forever letter gives us the opportunity to do so.

THE PROCESS OF WRITING CAN TAKE US TO THE HEART OF THE MATTER

When someone asks if he can record an audio or video version of his forever letter, I say "absolutely," because I understand that there's something visceral about hearing the voice of and/or seeing the image of someone we love that brings that person near to us. But I strongly believe that recording a forever letter should not take the place of writing one, especially when we consider the speed at which technology becomes obsolete.

Maybe this has happened to you. You begin to write an essay, a speech, or even a journal entry. You have your idea, your topic all mapped out; but after a few pages you find yourself heading down a very different path, in a direction you hadn't intended. That's what happens when we write. We operate at a slower pace and thus have time to think more deeply about what we feel. I know that sometimes I don't understand what I feel until I write it down. Sitting at a keyboard or with pen in hand doesn't necessarily guarantee automatic self-discovery, but it does indicate that we're ready to begin the process of clarifying who we are and what we stand for.

Neil and his wife, Susan, were living and working in Hong Kong before the birth of their first and only child. Wanting to find an outlet for their powerful emotions, articulate their feelings about becoming parents, create a "road map," and express their hopes for their child-to-be, Neil wrote a letter, on behalf of himself and his wife, to the being that yet resided in his wife's womb.

How to begin? This is where Neil's writing took him:

Dear Unborn Child,

You will arrive soon. Neither your Mother nor I are fully prepared for you. We are waiting for you a little like we wait for a typhoon here in Hong Kong. When a typhoon approaches the city, the Royal Observatory hoists a "signal" identified by a number. A "signal 1" means that there is a storm within a certain distance of the city but which may never come close enough for us to notice that it exists. As the storm approaches closer, a "signal 3" is hoisted and we usually feel some of the typhoon's weather. When the typhoon is certain to hit, a "signal 8" is raised.

A "signal 8" is flying for you, child. We know that you are coming.

Typhoon means "big wind" in Chinese and the Chinese believe that circumstances that occur at a time of a typhoon can be propitious. *Propitious* to the Chinese, like so many other things in your birth place, can mean many things, good and bad, little and big, but it certainly means change. People look for symbols in Asia to predict the future. How will things turn out?

Your mother and I wonder these things about you. How will you be? How good will we be as your parents? Will you arrive safely? You are our personal typhoon.

In the body of the letter, Neil wrote about their beliefs and hopes: the importance of friends and family, learning to share life with people we love, recognizing "sadness and tears as part of the same cloth as laughter," curiosity, valuing life, rejecting "violence and causing pain to others," having "the strength to care for others," asking for help when feeling afraid, and being true to oneself.

He concluded his letter by returning to the theme of the typhoon.

"After a typhoon, people build new things. If wisely done, the best of the old is restored and repaired and the worst is rejected and replaced. We expect you to change us and our lives, but we don't know how or in what ways. We are waiting for you, as yet unborn, little 'big wind'."

I imagine that when Neil sat down to write this letter, he had a sense of where he was headed, but I also imagine that, as he wrote, he came to better understand, and perhaps even discover, what it was that he truly wanted to say.

The same was true for Janine, a spunky eighty-one-year-old, who at the conclusion of a writing workshop, told the group that she used to be a triathlete and that to this day she has a bumper sticker on her car (a present from one of her daughters) that says, "Sill Running." Janine said this statement still defines her: she is someone who is always running. She then shared an epiphany she had as she reflected on her experience of writing. She said that she has been running so much, maybe too much, and that now she needs to stop and listen and tend to some things and some relationships in her life that need tending to.

Writing a forever letter offers us the opportunity to access our innermost selves, to see ourselves as honestly as we can, and to articulate our thoughts for ourselves and for the people we love. There's something about the act of writing that can get us to the heart of the matter.

WE CAN CLARIFY OUR VALUES AND LIVE WITH GREATER INTENTION

At some point during our lives, many of us struggle to define ourselves. We question who we are, the choices we've made, the values we've chosen to live. Sometimes we're catapulted into these moments by the loss of a job, depression, marriage, the acknowledgment of a drug or alcohol addiction, the birth of a child, an anniversary, a divorce, an illness, a death, becoming middle-aged, or retirement. Other times, perhaps a book, an exhibit, a conversation, a job offer, a poem, or time in the woods takes us there.

Author, teacher, and activist Parker Palmer writes about how the experience of being asked to become president of a small educational institution helped him clarify his values. To decide whether or not he should take the job, Palmer convened a "clearness committee," a custom in the Quaker community to get clarity on an issue. The clearness committee is a "group [of close friends that] refrains from giving you advice but spends three hours asking you honest, open questions to help you discover your own inner truth." [9] The deep listening and long periods of silence provided by this group enabled Palmer to see that this job wasn't right for him, and how just the thought of it somehow compromised his soul. Saying no to this job gave Palmer the opportunity to choose a different path, a path that would free him to live his values with intention.

We don't have to be Quakers to convene a "clearness committee" to process experiences that trouble us, that enable us to clarify our values or our inner truth. To learn more about how to convene a clearness committee, see Palmer's article, "The Clearness Committee," available online at the Center for Courage & Renewal. [10]

About five years after I moved to Seattle, my friend Linda gave me a gift much like a "clearness committee." I had been thinking about starting an alternative Jewish community because I missed being a congregational rabbi, but I also wanted more flexibility and freedom in my life. When I

---

9   Parker J. Palmer, *Let Your Life Speak: Listening for the Voice of Vocation* (San Francisco: Jossey-Bass, 2000), 44–45.

10   Parker J. Palmer, "The Clearness Committee: A Communal Approach to Discernment," Center for Courage and Renewal, www.couragerenewal.org /clearnesscommittee/.

mentioned this to Linda she told me to gather a group of friends and colleagues whom I trusted and respected, and to invite them to her house for lunch. She said that she would invite her consultant friend to facilitate. Her goal was to help me move forward.

So, I organized a group of colleagues and friends, one of whom flew to Seattle for the occasion. Through this process, it became clear to me that starting a community wasn't what I *really* wanted to do. I *really* wanted to put my energy into writing and I *really* wanted the flexibility to be more present as a mother to my son who was then in elementary school. At that time, though I didn't give myself permission to write as often as I would have liked, I was at least able to honor a voice within me that said, "Respect your soul's desire. Don't be drawn in by people who admire you and who want you to start a community. Be true to your values. Live with your intention in mind."

While sitting in silence wasn't part of my clearness-like committee experience, this gathering of women enabled me to shut out the noise of the outer world long enough to listen to my inner voice. Tuning into our inner voice is part of the experience of writing a forever letter. The difference is that no one is there to help us clarify our values, to remind us to be honest with ourselves, or to suggest to us that we live more consistently with our values. When we write, we have only ourselves to rely on, but we *do have* ourselves, and we have the power of our voice, our truth, and the writing process.

As we write a forever letter, we may find ourselves asking questions that help us further clarify our values, questions such as: Who am I? How do I show up in the world? Am I living the values I want to live? Am I living the values I think I'm living? Do I always act in accordance with my values, or do I blow it? Do I deliver empty promises, or do I follow through on what I say I will do? Do I reach out to those in need, or do I hold back? Am I there for my children when they need me, or only when I need them to need me? Am I there for my parents when they need me, or only when I need them? Am I there for my aunts and uncles, siblings, partner, spouse, friends? Do I listen—*really* listen—when someone sits before me in pain, or do I zone out because really listening is just too hard? Do I make time for family, or do I just speak about how important family time is? Do I maintain a healthy life-work balance? Can I play or is my life all about work? Do I let my work stress invade my home life and influence the way I treat the people I love?

I asked myself many of these questions when my son was six and a half and I wrote him a forever letter. As I wrote about what was most important to me—love, compassion, forgiveness, faith, tradition, and charity—I realized the painful truth: that I wasn't as consistent in living these values as I wanted to be, that I wasn't the near-perfect mother I imagined I would be, and that I wasn't living my values often enough in Gabriel's presence for him to understand how much a part of me they truly are. Writing to Gabriel enabled me to see that I had fallen short and that I had work to do to better align my life with my values. Writing to Gabriel gave me the opportunity to reclaim values I cared about and let go of values I did not.

I understand that my values may not be Gabriel's values, and that one day he will articulate his own values; but by imparting to him the values that I believe in and struggle to live, I articulate the importance of living with values.

We all fall short. Yet, if we're honest with ourselves and we're able to admit that a value we once held dear is less important to us than it once had been, we can let it go; or if we notice that a value remains important to us, we can recommit ourselves to living this value with greater intent.

WE CAN ASK FOR FORGIVENESS AND WE CAN FORGIVE

When we begin to clarify our values and ask ourselves many of the questions we just asked ourselves, we begin to see the things for which we may want to forgive others, ask forgiveness from others, and, most important, forgive ourselves. Writing a forever letter can give us the opportunity to work on these aspects of forgiveness.

As I contemplate writing another forever letter to Gabriel, my mistakes tumble around inside me. I think back to that night in his bedroom when he was almost two. The room is dark except for the night-light and the soft yellow shadow of the hall light. Gabriel, blue-eyed with blond curls, is standing in his crib in his yellow onesie. He is whining. I am standing next to his crib yelling at him. My voice is angry. He looks at me, as if to say, "Who is this mommy that I thought I knew? Why is she so angry?" Tears form in the corners of his eyes and roll down his cheeks. I sit on the green glider next to his crib and rest my head in my hands. "I'm sorry I yelled," I say. "I'm angry, but I should not have yelled at you. It's not okay." Gabriel looks at me with confused eyes as he musters all the strength he has stored up in that little body of his, and says, "Mama, don't do dat again." I lift him from the crib, hug him, place him back into the crib, and tell him that Daddy is going to finish putting him to sleep. I walk into my husband's home office, and I ask him to take over; then I walk into our bedroom, sit on our bed, and cry, contemplating what a terrible mother I am, so terrible I do not deserve to be a mother at all.

Some years ago Donna, a writer friend, then fifty-eight, with two grown daughters, ages twenty-four and thirty, e-mailed me this reflection on motherhood after reading an earlier draft of a section of this book: "I am at the stage of motherhood where I am reviewing all that I did wrong. Those 3 a.m. tossing and turnings where I relive my worst moments. Did I really slap my daughter's face once in the throes of a mother-daughter adolescent war when she called me a bitch? My face still burns at the thought. Fortunately, in spite of me, I have two wonderful loving adult daughters but the idea of writing [a forever letter] [11] is powerful. It would

---

11   Brackets indicate my change of *ethical will* to *forever letter*.

mean acknowledging that I did not always live up to my ideal as a mother, and what high ideals I had starting out. I was going to do it all, demanding career and homemade organic food each night at dinner. I have been humbled. I think parenthood is one of those tasks that we are set up to fail. Does any parent feel that they got it right all the time?"

As parents, most of us realize we don't get it right all the time and we're lucky if we get it right seventy-five percent of the time. We remember those awful parenting moments that continue to haunt us and those awful day-to-day moments when we could have responded more lovingly or more compassionately than we did.

In "The Eighth Sacrament," Oregon author Tricia Gates Brown writes about those awful day-to-day moments. According to Brown, her failures as a mother began on the third day of motherhood when she lost her patience with her colicky daughter, Madison. Her failures as a mother continued on through the years, when she silenced Madison during the concerts and classes Madison had been too young to attend, and when she nagged Madison to organize her room "before learning Madison had a brain ill-equipped for organization." And what about the times she withdrew into silence instead of being present for her daughter who needed her? Brown does not let herself off the hook easily. She admits her failures and she asks for forgiveness. [12]

In a letter to his son, physician and poet William Carlos Williams writes about an awful parenting moment that continues to haunt him. It happened one summer when his son, William Eric, was about to win a canoe race at camp, but didn't, because someone unfairly cut him off. This caused William Eric to burst into tears. Instead of empathizing, William Carlos Williams laughed. About this moment of shame he writes, "I like a God damned fool laughed at you. Why? Just to hide my own

---

12   Tricia Gates Brown, "The Eighth Sacrament," *The University of Portland Magazine* 32, no. 1 (Spring 2013): 18.

embarrassment. You looked at me and said, 'It was my only chance to win anything!' I tell you that hurt. I've never forgotten it. Such are a father's inner regrets."[13]

Marian Wright Edelman, founder and president of the Children's Defense Fund, reached out and asked for her sons' forgiveness in *The Measure of Our Success: A Letter to My Children and Yours*. She writes: "I seek your forgiveness for all the times I talked when I should have listened; got angry when I should have been patient; acted when I should have waited; feared when I should have delighted; scolded when I should have encouraged; criticized when I should have complimented; said no when I should have said yes and said yes when I should have said no. I did not know a whole lot about parenting or how to ask for help."[14]

As parents, forgiving ourselves is probably one of the hardest things to do, but we can; and we can also reach out and seek forgiveness from our children whom we have hurt. When we ask our children for forgiveness, we can admit that we have failed them, that we have failed ourselves, and that we hope not to fail them this way in the future. While our apology may not dissolve their hurt or anger, it does present us as human and fallible, which is important for our children to see. It also models for them the importance and the power of asking for forgiveness, and may encourage them to do the same when they feel they are at fault.

None of us is perfect, not in our role as parents, nor in any of the other roles we inhabit. On occasion, we lose it, we act in ways that embarrass or disgust us, we hurt someone's feelings, or we say the wrong thing. We want to know that despite our imperfections, or perhaps *because* of them,

---

13 William Carlos Williams to William Eric Williams, September 25, 1942, in *The Selected Letters of William Carlos Williams*, ed. John C. Thirlwall (New York: McDowell, Obolensky, 1957), 201. Also in Dorie McCullough Lawson, *Posterity: Letters of Great Americans to Their Children* (New York: Doubleday, 2004), 117–118.

14 Marian Wright Edelman, *The Measure of Our Success: A Letter to My Children and Yours* (New York: HarperPerennial, 1993), 27–28.

we're still worthy of love. Isn't that our biggest fear, that our failures render us unlovable?

That was Dalia's fear. Dalia, in her nineties, was grappling with something she had done for which she could not forgive herself. What exactly it was, I don't know. She was too ashamed to tell me—but whatever it was hurt, shamed, embarrassed her, and made her feel so unworthy that her body shook as she spoke. All she could say was something like: Just hold my hand and tell me I'm a good person. I did as she asked, understanding full well that even by telling her she was a good person, removing the hurt from her heart was something only she could do.

The good news is that, if we're fundamentally good and kind, if we've built up enough love and trust in ourselves, we can get to the point we're able to forgive ourselves. As we navigate this journey of forgiveness, we may find that sometimes we must forgive ourselves before seeking forgiveness from another, and that other times we must seek forgiveness from another before we're able to forgive ourselves.

The latter happened to me years ago when I was teaching an adult education class of forty to fifty people. As often happens, there were two to three students who always participated. When they did, I noticed others in the class move uncomfortably in their chairs, annoyed that these individuals were taking up all the airtime. I tried to manage the class by inviting more participation from others. Apparently, I wasn't doing a good job. One day after class, Maggie, one of the students I had tried to hold back, confronted me. I wasn't calling on her. I was avoiding her. She cried and yelled. She yelled some more. I did what I had to do. I listened. When she let go of all her anger, I apologized. I told her that I wasn't aware of how much I had been putting her off, that my intention had not been to hurt her but enable others to participate. I told her that I was sorry I had caused her so much pain, that I hoped she would forgive me, that I would do better.

On the rare occasion that our paths still cross, Maggie and I have more than a cordial connection. There's a bond between us. That bond is there because I acknowledged her feelings and asked for her forgiveness. Forgiving myself came later as I processed our conversation and began to think about her words, and how I could have better handled the situation.

Chris, a nurse I admire, told me that some years back when his mother was ill and unable to care for herself, he brought her from the Philippines to the United States to care for her. His sister couldn't be there to help because she lived in London and had a family of her own. Chris understood. He never blamed his sister for not being around, but after their mother died, whenever he and his sister spoke on the phone, all she kept telling him was that he should have done more. Chris knew his sister's words came from a place of guilt, being unable to forgive herself for not being there to help him care for their mother at the end of her life. Still, her words stung. He told her she could blame him if she wanted, but he knew he had done all he could.

Chris didn't carry a grudge. He knew his sister was hurting. Instead, he prayed and he meditated that she would come to understand. About a year after their mother's death, his sister called to apologize and to thank him for all he had done. Chris cried. No, he said, he bawled. He forgave his sister. He told her he had no bad feelings toward her. He knew she hadn't been able to come to the United States because her family was in Europe, and he assured her that their mother knew this, too.

All relationships, even healthy relationships, need work. Most of us have things for which we need to forgive ourselves, people from whom we need to ask for forgiveness, and people we need to forgive. But do we? How often do we push ourselves to do this important work? It seems to me that all too often we're content to remain in the safe zone, in that state of in-between-ness, afraid to make a move, afraid to upset the status quo we have come to accept as normal.

The actress, director, producer, and writer Mary Pickford got it right when she said, "However, if you have made mistakes, even serious mistakes, there is always another chance for you. And supposing you have tried and failed again and again, you may have a fresh start any moment you choose, for this thing we call 'failure' is not the falling down, but the staying down."[15]

We don't have to stay down. We can change the status quo. We can take action.

In one of my workshops, Camila, in her mid-sixties, spoke about how she had taken action in her relationship with her father, who had quit being an alcoholic when she was twelve, only to begin drinking again seven years later, and at that time drank so much he almost died. She carried this hurt and sadness with her for many years, and over the years wrote him many angry letters that she never mailed. As time passed, however, her anger toward him softened and she found herself moving toward compassion. She began to feel sad for him, sad that he had missed out on being a father. So, one day, she wrote him a letter that she actually mailed. She wrote something like, *I've been sorting out my life and my being angry with you. I feel sad you missed out on being my dad. I'm sorry you were hurting so much you couldn't be there. I'm okay. I forgive you. I love you.*

Camila said her dad wrote back almost immediately, apologizing that it had taken him so long to respond. He hadn't said he was sorry. He hadn't said much of anything, but she chose to understand his immediate response as an apology. She also said that when she received his letter she understood that, though she forgave him, he would still have to find a way to forgive himself.

In another workshop, Robert talked about how his seventy-five-year-old estranged father with whom he had a difficult relationship had taken

---

15   Mary Pickford, "Why Not Try God?" *St. Petersburg Times*, sect. 2, January 25, 1936, 3.

action by writing him a letter. His father reported that he had been diagnosed with a terminal illness, didn't think he'd be around much longer, and asked to meet up with his son. Robert thought about his father's request for a while before responding in the affirmative. Though they always had issues, they remained connected until his father died. Here's the amazing thing: Robert's father lived to the age of ninety-four. I believe that once he and Robert connected, he was able to clear away some of the guilt that had weighed so heavily upon him it had literally been making him sick. Others in the room felt similarly.

The Mayo Clinic says in an article entitled "10 Tips for Better Health": "Take conscious steps to forgive those closest to you—and yourself. Forgiveness is associated with improved mood and lower stress." [16]

Dr. Fred Luskin, cofounder and director of the Stanford Forgiveness Project and author of *Forgive for Good* writes: "People who are more forgiving report fewer health problems." [17]

Heavy emotional baggage from old hurts that we have inflicted or that we have suffered can weigh us down and even make us sick. Letting go of this baggage, forgiving ourselves, asking for forgiveness, and granting forgiveness can make us healthier and can lengthen our lives.

I must tell one final story about forgiveness that not only incorporates the shortest forever letter I have yet discovered, but highlights the intense power of forgiveness for both the person who forgives and for the person being forgiven. Almost every time I tell this story my eyes fill with tears, my voice shakes, and I have to pause a few times in the telling. When I look out at my audience, I see that I am not alone.

---

16   "10 Tips for Better Health," Mayo Clinic News Network, May 4, 2011, www
.businesswire.com/news/home/20110505006693/en/Mayo-Clinic-Health-Letter
-2011-Highlights-10.

17   Fred Luskin, *Forgive for Good: A Proven Prescription for Health and Happiness* (New
York: HarperSanFrancisco, 2002), xv.

Some years ago in *Guideposts Magazine*, nurse Sue Kidd wrote about an experience she had tending to a man who had a heart attack and who asked her to call his daughter, Janie, his only relative. When Sue called, Janie told her that she and her dad had an awful quarrel and hadn't seen one another for close to a year. Janie spoke about wanting to ask for her father's forgiveness, but never followed through. She said that the last words she had said to him were, "I hate you." Janie raced to the hospital, but she arrived too late. Distraught, she asked if she could see her dad. Sue took her to his room, and as Janie "buried her face in her father's sheets," Sue noticed a scrap of paper. She picked it up. On it were these words: "My dearest Janie, I forgive you. I pray you will also forgive me. I know that you love me. I love you, too. Daddy." [18]

I'm in awe of this father who had the presence of mind to leave a note of forgiveness for his daughter. It's clear he understood that without his note, she would likely have trouble forgiving herself. I'm in awe of him for yet another reason. He apologized to his daughter for his responsibility in their rift. He understood that a rift takes two and that he also needed to be forgiven.

Over the years in my role as rabbi, chaplain, and teacher, I've heard many stories of unresolved hurt within families—between brothers and sisters, parents and children, husbands and wives, and others—so many hurts it feels like a plague. I understand that there are situations of extreme abuse, neglect, violence, or deceit; that there are situations when someone has caused a hurt that she takes no responsibility for and cares nothing about, and so how can we forgive someone who doesn't believe she needs to be forgiven; that there are situations still too open, too raw, and too new to know how to handle; that there are situations in which thinking about asking for forgiveness or thinking about forgiving feels impossible

---

18   Sue Kidd, "Don't Let It End This Way," *Guidepost Magazine* Nov 2006, vol. 61, issue 9, 80.

to imagine, and maybe it is, but consider the alternative: living with the hurt and having the hurt fester inside us until we die.

The beauty of writing a forever letter is that it gives us the opportunity to forgive ourselves, to ask for forgiveness, and to forgive the persons to whom we're writing. As we write, we can ask ourselves these questions: What heavy baggage do I still carry that I must lay to rest? What load do I need to lighten so that I can live without guilt and regret? What am I waiting for? And we have a choice. We can leave our forever letter to be found after our death, in a place where it can be easily discovered, such as in a dresser drawer, bedside table, home office next to important papers, or in our safe deposit box (but we must let our family or close friends know that we have a safe deposit box and leave them a key); or we can hand it over while we're still alive, like my father did, to create an understanding or to open up a conversation that can be crucial in any circumstance, but particularly crucial when we've written to someone asking for forgiveness or offering forgiveness, as it gives us a chance to reconcile and possibly even to reclaim that relationship.

WE CAN MAKE OURSELVES KNOWN

I was facilitating a writing workshop in a tight-knit community that was used to learning together. There were seventy-five people in the room whose ages ranged from twelve to eighty-something. Deidre, in her late forties, spoke. She said that her dad had died when he was sixty-one and that he hadn't written a forever letter. She went on to talk about how she loved her father and how she knew her father loved her, but she lamented not knowing more about what was really going on in his heart because he had been so quiet. Her takeaway: she would write a forever letter to her children so that they would know what was going on in her heart.

In another writing workshop, Jill, in her late fifties, spoke about how both of her parents had died, and had left her with some money, a statue, and other material goods, but how empty that felt, and how she didn't want that to be her legacy to her children.

If you come from a family where your parents didn't speak much about their history, their lives, or their feelings, maybe you can understand how much of a void can be created when a loved one does not make him- or herself known.

Ruth Reichl, in *Not Becoming My Mother and Other Things She Taught Me along the Way*, writes about discovering a box of her mother's letters and notes after her mother's death, and how reading her mother's words enabled her to better understand and appreciate her grandparents, her father, and especially her mother, with whom she had a strained relationship. She came to know her mother at different stages in her mother's life, from childhood to adulthood, and to see the woman behind the mother she knew—a woman who "was more thoughtful, more self-aware and much more generous" than she had understood her to be, a woman who had hopes and dreams—but who for various reasons was unable to live them. She came to understand how much she owed her mother, whose "enormous emotional sacrifices" enabled her to live the life she lives today. "Getting to know her now," Reichl writes, "I realized how much I missed by not knowing her better when she was still alive." [19] Reading the notes and letters in this box also gave Reichl the opportunity to remember her mother more positively. Had her mother been more transparent, perhaps they would have had a closer relationship.

Unlike Reichl, who learned more about her mother after her mother's death, author Jung Chang learned about her mother from her mother directly, who, one day, began to tell Chang her story, a story she had kept hidden for years. With Chang's interest and encouragement her mother recorded sixty hours of her life history into a tape recorder, and Chang

---

19 Ruth Reichl, *Not Becoming My Mother and Other Things She Taught Me along the Way* (New York: Penguin, 2009), 17–18.

used this information to write *Wild Swans*, a three-generational biography about the women in her family and their lives in China beginning in the early 1900s. It is in a letter to her granddaughter that Chang writes about how her experience hearing these stories helped her to understand her history, fill in the missing pieces of her childhood, and "develop a new degree of respect and love for [her] mother." Her hope is that reading *Wild Swans* would do the same for her granddaughter. [20]

Steve Jobs had a similar idea. When asked by his biographer, Walter Isaacson, why he was willing to "open up so much for a book when he was usually so private," Jobs said, "I wanted my kids to know me. I wasn't always there for them, and I wanted them to know why and to understand what I did." [21]

Do you always understand why people do the things they do? Why they say the things they say? I don't, and I'm often struck by the fact that I don't, that sometimes I understand people's actions or words differently than they intend for their words or actions to be understood. We don't always make ourselves easily understood. Maybe it's because we're ashamed of our feelings, because we're not clear in our own minds how we feel, or because we assume that others can read our minds, so why bother stating what's perfectly clear? But we must explain ourselves, especially to the people we love, as the easiest opportunities for misunderstandings are with the people we love most.

By explaining ourselves, I don't mean just information sharing, I mean expressing emotions and love. There are times that we're not transparent with our emotions or with our love. Couched in this next story that my uncle Charles told me about himself and his fiancée is the realization that his father loved him. In 1962, when he was twenty-two and dating Rebecca,

---

20   Jung Chang, "Dear Granddaughter," in *Letter to My Grandchild*, ed. Liv Ullmann (New York: Atlantic Monthly Press, 1998), 18.

21   Walter Isaacson, "American Icon," *Time*, October 17, 2011, 25.

the woman who would become his wife, he enlisted in the army. Before heading off to basic training, he wanted to make Rebecca a gift, to leave her with something he had created in case he never returned.

He spent hours in his basement workshop carving a wooden bowl, but when he put the pumice powder on the wood to make it smooth and shiny, the bowl split, jumped off the lathe, fell on the floor, and busted into pieces. Devastated, he switched off the lathe, turned off the basement light, and went up to bed. On his way, he made a passing remark to his father about breaking the bowl. "I wonder if it's a sign," he said. A bad omen is what he meant.

My uncle recalls going down to the basement the next morning to find a mended wooden bowl sitting on his worktable. He understood that his father had stayed up late into the night to repair it, and he was filled with gratitude, not only because his bowl had been mended, but because it was his father who had mended it. Since his father hadn't been transparent with his love, my uncle said that this was the first time he understood, really understood, that his father loved him. Today that wooden bowl sits on his bookshelf and reminds him of his father's love.

According to my uncle, the only time his father used the word *love* when speaking to him or to my mother was when he would say, "You don't have to love me, but you do have to respect me." My uncle said that even on his father's deathbed, when he held one of his father's hands and my mother held the other, all their father was able to say to them was, "You're good kids." Now in his seventies, my uncle still mourns the loss of his father's ability to say, "I love you."

As parents, we can write a forever letter as a way to explain to our children why we chose to send them to a public school rather than the private school attended by many of their friends, why we decided to raise them in a small town rather than in a city, and we can also explain to them why we were angry for much of their childhood, how we parented them the best we could given the abusive home from which we came, why we drank, why we were afraid to tell them how much we loved them or that we really, truly did love them.

While the examples in this section highlight making ourselves known as parents to our children, we, as children, can also make ourselves known. We can write a forever letter as a way to explain to our parents why we chose to postpone college, why we decided to marry the person we married even though they disapproved, why we decided not to have children, or why we decided to vote for a different presidential candidate.

As a partner or spouse, we can write a forever letter to make ourselves known to our lover. We can write as a way to explain why we're afraid to love deeply, what prevents us from being as honest as we would like, why sex is uncomfortable, why it's hard to say, "I love you."

We can make ourselves known to all the people in our life whom we love to whom we have not yet made ourselves known. Have we told the people we love about us? Have we explained ourselves? Have we been transparent with our love? If we haven't, it's time. What do we need to tell the people we love about us so that they can better understand us, themselves, and our relationship? Writing a forever letter gives us the opportunity to make ourselves known.

WE CAN COME TO BETTER UNDERSTAND OURSELVES AND OUR RELATIONSHIPS

In the process of explaining ourselves to others, we often come to better understand ourselves and our relationships. We see qualities in ourselves that we like and qualities that we dislike. We see qualities we want to let go of and qualities we want to hold onto. Writing changes us, gives us the opportunity to make changes in ourselves, and opens up the possibility for us to make changes in our relationships.

I had this experience when I was writing a speech to deliver at Park Avenue Synagogue in New York when I returned for a weekend as a scholar-in-residence. One of the topics I was asked to speak on was "The Sacred Spark: Why I Am a Jew in the Twenty-First Century." In this speech, I spoke about my parents and my grandparents, for it was their wisdom, guidance, love of Judaism, and love of me that helped to instill Judaism within me.

I usually e-mail my speeches to my parents for their feedback. This speech was no different. My father's response: "It's good." My mother's response: "It's okay." Usually their feedback was more in sync. Why the disparity? I wasn't sure, but I soon learned.

On the Thursday before I delivered the speech, my father spoke to me at the round table in their New York City time-share (that they maintained for a number of years after my father's retirement) while my mother fixed lunch in the kitchen a few feet away. They had driven in from Baltimore to spend the weekend in New York to hear me speak on Saturday morning. With kindness and compassion, my father pointed out that the words I had written about my mother didn't do her justice. "Why is that?" he asked. He didn't ask the question expecting me to answer. He didn't want me to answer. He encouraged me to explore the issue. He wanted me to look deep within and think about why it was hard for me to write a paragraph about my mother. He suggested that my mother was more present to me than anyone he knew.

My father's words resonated. I knew I hadn't done my mother justice. But it wasn't until his reproach that I was able to come up with the right words. I left my parents' apartment, walked down the hall to my apartment, and rewrote the paragraph about my mother. Out the words poured, so effortlessly, as if they had been on the page all along.

But they hadn't. What had stopped them from emerging? Why hadn't I been able to access them earlier? Why had I needed a reproach from my father to find them? I would contemplate these questions in therapy one day, but, at that moment, I had work to do. I wanted to apologize to my mother for hurting her feelings. It was clear why she hadn't given my speech a better review. It wasn't the speech as a whole that gave her pause, it was the paragraph I had written about her.

After I rewrote the paragraph, I copied it out for her on a separate piece of paper along with a letter of apology. I told her that when I returned to Seattle, I would input the revision into my computer and e-mail it to her. Here is the revised version that I later adapted to weave into the first forever letter I wrote to Gabriel: "My mother's love for me was constant and total. No matter what I did. No matter how I felt about myself. Her love was, and is, ever-present. 'I will be with you,' said God to Moses at the burning bush. 'I will accompany you on your way. You will never be alone.' My mother's love and her presence gave me a sense of security, not only to face my own challenges, but to face larger challenges in the world."

I had hoped to include my earlier version here to show the difference between the two and how far I had come. I had also hoped to find the earlier version to see if there was anything I could ascertain, such as a clue about why I had held back. After searching through my hard copies and my computer files, I found only the edited version; the only version I wanted to remember.

I guess you could say that it wasn't quite the writing of this speech that enabled me to better understand my relationship with my mother, rather it was my father who read what I had written and encouraged me to think about why I had such difficulty, and that would be true; but I believe that the reason I was so receptive to his words was because he helped me attune to the feeling—I hadn't done my mother justice—that I sensed on a gut level.

I've always loved both my parents, but it was my father whom I considered myself most like, admired, and wanted to grow up to be. I didn't want to grow up to be my mother, at home raising kids, cooking, cleaning, washing clothes, carting four kids around, entertaining guests, and proofreading sermons. I wanted to be out in the world creating meaning for others. As a child coming of age in the early seventies, I spent much of my life as a tomboy, lamenting being born a girl. I somehow understood that my options were limited. I had a sense that my father got the better deal, that society respected his work in the world more than my mother's work in the home, and that his job as a rabbi was a "want to" while my mother's job as a homemaker was a "have to."

That's not how my mother saw it. In the mid-fifties when she was finishing college, her career options were limited. She had no desire to be a lawyer like her father, nor did she desire to be her mother—a woman who spent most days running around with her mother, and leaving her children to be raised as she was, by live-in nannies.

My mother's desire was to marry my father (whom she met in her mid-teens), to become a mother, and to raise her own children. She also wanted to do something important in the world as long as it didn't prevent her from raising her children. At one point, when she was in college at Brandeis, she had thought about becoming an artist but tabled the thought because she knew it would take too much time away from raising children. As she saw it, she had two options: nursing and teaching. She chose teaching because it gave her the flexibility to spend summers with us.

This model worked for my mother, in part, because it was what she had chosen and, in part, because she received so much love and appreciation from my father, who often announced that she was his strength and that he was able to do all he did because of her. It also worked because she had many hobbies. To this day, I can still see my mother sitting in what she called her "sewing room" at her Singer sewing machine crafting clothes and beanbags for us, and, some years later, in the same room, working on her assignments for her calligraphy classes. How she loved to be alone in this "room of her own," giving voice to her creative spirit. We were all so happy for her when, at the age of sixty-six, she received her Master of Fine Arts from the Maryland Institute College of Art, rented studio space, and began to exhibit her work.

As time goes on, I see how much like my mother I am: how her creative spirit is so much a part of my soul I would be lost without it, how after my son was born, I chose part-time work to be able to have more flexibility, how I have succeeded in honoring my creative spirit more in my later years, and how I continue to maintain a room of my own.

Just as writing this speech enabled me to begin to revisit myself, to better understand my relationship with my mother, and to understand that our relationship needed work, so writing a forever letter can help us to better understand ourselves and our relationships, and can offer us the opportunity to change the course of our relationships.

WE CAN STATE OUR ULTIMATE TRUTH

While it's true that the process of writing a forever letter can lead us to self discovery, it's also true that we can write a forever letter to communicate our ultimate truth, the truth that resides deep within us, and that we are able to more fully comprehend toward the end of our lives as we begin to reflect on the whole of our lives. When we sense our mortality, ready ourselves to meet our maker, and contemplate taking leave of this world and of the people we love, honesty and truth are all we have left. To write a forever letter at this stage in our lives is to take the courageous step of writing down this ultimate truth for ourselves and for the people we love.

An example of a man who states his ultimate truth can be found in the heartwarming Japanese movie, *Riding Alone for Thousands of Miles*. Kenichi, a young man who has been estranged from his father for many years, is in the hospital ill from cancer. His wife, Rie, sensing that her husband doesn't have long to live, phones her father-in-law, Gouichi, and asks him to come to see his son. Gouichi leaves his fishing village and travels to the city, but when he arrives at the hospital Kenichi refuses to see him. Rie, who is trying to reunite them, feels bad. She cannot send her father-in-law off empty-handed, so she gives him a video of Kenichi's life's work. Gouichi watches this video as soon as he returns home. He learns that Kenichi is passionate about Chinese folk operas, and that when Kenichi had last been in China filming these operas, he had promised to return the following year to film a certain folk opera. Upon discovering this, Gouichi sets off to China to film this folk opera as a gift for his dying son.

When Gouichi is in China, Rie phones him a few times to update him on Kenichi's failing health. Gouichi expresses concern, though he doesn't seem to want to believe that Kenichi will die before he returns to Japan, folk opera in hand. The dreaded call comes. Rie tells her father-in-law that Kenichi died. She reports that before Kenichi died he was talking about his father and wanted to write his father a letter. Rie reads Gouichi that letter.

What do I want to say? "What should I say to my father?" I'm asking myself. I deeply regret refusing to see you when you came to the hospital. This feeling of regret torments me more than my illness. I've been blaming you ever since Mother's death. Without any explanation, you moved away to a remote fishing village. I thought then you were trying to avoid facing reality. To be honest, I've been trying to escape it as well. When you came to the hospital, I couldn't face the distance between us. I never expected that you would ever go to China for me. I was really moved. People have never understood my obsession with folk operas. I've been drawn to them because they mirror my life. I've come to realize that I'm the actor behind the mask. I've tried to fool myself and everyone close to me. My true feelings have eluded me until now. I have not allowed myself to acknowledge them. Father, it's not the opera that is important. I now see that loved ones should not mask their true feelings for one another. I eagerly wait for your return. Father, I want us to embrace each other once again. [22]

---

22 *Riding Alone for Thousands of Miles,* directed by Yimou Zhang and Yasuo Furuhata (2007; United States: Sony Pictures Classics, 2005), DVD.

Hearing that his father had traveled to China to film the folk opera that he had hoped to return to China to film himself moved Kenichi deeply, especially after he had refused to see his father, who had traveled to the city and to the hospital specifically to see him. That Kenichi wrote his ultimate truth in a letter to his father, that he acknowledged his father's love, and that he expressed his love to his father was a blessing for himself and for his father.

Toward the end of life, as we face our mortality, we often can ask ourselves hard questions. Questions like: What was my ultimate truth? Did I live it? How have I succeeded? How have I failed? Now consider this question: Can I write my ultimate truth in a forever letter to the people I love? For me? For them? For our relationship?

WE CAN INFLUENCE THE WAY WE WILL BE REMEMBERED

Leo was in his early eighties when I first met him. He had a booming voice and a positive personality; he would wax on about his life, community, and family, often quoting his grandfather, a pivotal figure in his life. He always had stories to tell and love to impart. At eighty-six, as he lay in his nursing home bed dying of cancer, as oxygen flowed into his nostrils, and as morphine numbed his pain, he held court as family and friends came to say goodbye.

On one of my visits, his wife, Ruby, had a hard time holding back her tears, and I, too, had a hard time holding back mine. I had come to love Leo, and I didn't want him to die. I had come to love Ruby, and I worried how she'd do without him. Yet as I listened to Leo speak, he was not angry or sad. He seemed so positive. I asked him if he was really as positive as he seemed, or if he was just putting it on for me, the rabbi.

Leo said: "I'm grateful for the years I've been given. It hasn't been easy for my wife, my sons, or my grandchildren. They're all hurting. But why should everyone be sad? I must give them hope. I'm not going to be negative. What do I have to be negative about? It doesn't help. I've had a good life. If the only thing I take with me is what is good, what my children have given me, what my parents have given me, and what my grandparents have given me, I have nothing but blessings."

I was in awe. Leo was dying, yet he was so full of life. I turned to Ruby, who looked at me and nodded, confirming that this was, indeed, the way her husband chose to approach the end of his stay in this world.

Before I left, Leo gave me advice: "Go home every night and give that son of yours a hug and tell him of the love you have for him."

Leo spoke as if it might be the last time he'd see me. I wasn't ready. It was too soon. "I'll be back," I said, but he bid me farewell. "May you have a good life with joy and love in your heart."

I never saw Leo again.

To die so grateful, so full of life—what a legacy Leo left his family. What a legacy he left me.

Over one hundred years ago, Alfred Nobel established the Nobel Prizes in economics, medicine, science, literature, and peace. Nobel was an industrialist, engineer, and inventor who lived from 1833 to 1896. As an inventor, he obtained fifty-five patents in different medical fields. But his greatest invention, and the invention that made him wealthy and famous, was dynamite.

How did Nobel come to establish this prize? According to Harold Kushner by way of Joseph Telushkin, it happened because of someone's mistake. When one of Alfred's brothers died, a reporter mistakenly thought it was Alfred, and wrote Alfred's obituary. Alfred, very much alive, got to read his obituary and see himself portrayed as a man who had created a weapon of mass destruction. "At that moment," writes Telushkin, "Nobel realized two things: that this was how he was going to be remembered, and that this was *not* how he wanted to be remembered. Shortly thereafter, he established the awards. Today, because of his doing so, everyone is familiar with the Nobel Prize, while relatively few people even recall how Nobel made his fortune."[23]

This story should not teach us that we can manipulate our history to create a better legacy, but it can teach us that we may add to our legacy if it doesn't seem to reflect the whole of our values.

How does this story motivate us to write a forever letter? It reminds us to take stock of our lives and to ask ourselves if the way we've lived our lives up until this point is the way we want to be remembered. If the answer is yes, we can continue living the way we've been living. If the answer is no, we have to change. And fast!

---

23   Joseph Telushkin, *The Book of Jewish Values: A Day-by-Day Guide to Ethical Living* (New York: Bell Tower, 2000), 154–155.

3

WHY WE RESIST

Paralyze resistance with persistence.
—WOODY HAYES [24]

Many of us will immediately resonate with the concept of writing forever letters, but there are just as many of us who resist. In this chapter, I present and debunk the most popular reasons people offer for not writing. My hope is to convince the resisters among us to push through their resistance and to write.

"I'M NOT A WRITER."

"I'm not a writer," many people say to me. I nod in understanding and say, "You don't have to be a writer to write a forever letter. Just be yourself."

---

24 Qtd. in Dan Clark, *Weathering the Storm* (New York: British American Publishing, 1990), 125.

To write a forever letter, we don't have to have a flair for words. We don't have to be budding essayists, up-and-coming novelists, or potential poets. We don't have to be masters of metaphors, similes, appositives, gerunds, and adverbial clauses of manner.

Here's what we must be: people who have wisdom and love that we want to express, the courage and the desire to express them, and the confidence to do so. It's *our* voice, inflections, convictions, expressions, essence, values, wisdom, and love that the person we're writing to wants to hear.

The eighteenth-century Hasidic Master Rabbi Zusya of Hanipol understood this when he said, "In the coming world, they will not ask me: 'Why were you not Moses?' They will ask me: 'Why were you not Zusya?'" [25] Our goal in life is not to figure out how to be someone else but to figure out how to be ourselves. When we write a forever letter, we have only to be ourselves.

"I Have Nothing to Say."

"I've thought about writing a forever letter to my son, but I don't know what I'd say to him. He has surpassed me. He has a better work ethic than I do, and he's more conscientious than I ever was." These words were spoken by Carol, my mother-in-law, when she was sixty-seven. She was speaking about Seth, her only child, my husband.

Carol is far from thinking her son is perfect. She has no trouble acknowledging his faults and no trouble confronting him when she's disturbed by the way he's handling a situation. So, what is it about writing Seth that gives Carol pause? I think she wonders if he'll appreciate her words and take them to heart. You see, my mother-in-law and her son, while similar in many ways, occupy very different worlds. She spreads energy over him when he is out of sorts. Before he leaves on a trip, she asks

---

25   Martin Buber, *Tales of the Hasidim: The Early Masters* (New York: Schocken Books, 1975), 251.

him to place a small feather she gave him into his wallet for protection (a feather she claims has grown over time). On occasion, she converses with dead relatives, who offer her guidance. She inhabits a spirit world that her son is not privy to and does not understand.

Carol shouldn't worry. Yes, her son is more rational, conscientious, and has a better work ethic, and no, he doesn't understand her spiritual side. However, he loves his mother very much and will read whatever she writes, appreciating the values, guidance, and love she imparts. He will take to heart her thoughts and he will feel her love and he will be humbled when she writes that he has exceeded her expectations.

My mother-in-law is not alone. There are many parents (often immigrant parents, less-educated parents, parents unable to pursue their dreams) who feel as though their children have surpassed them. Many of these parents feel a sense of inferiority and a sense that their children may not respect them. To me, this is sad. I have found that most children respect their immigrant or less-educated parents for the strong values with which their parents raised them and for the opportunities that their parents' sacrifices have provided for them to achieve all they have.

It's not only some parents who feel as if they have nothing to say to their children. Sometimes children writing to their parents feel the same way. Imagine children who feel as if they've never quite made it in their parents' eyes. What do they have to offer to their parents who have succeeded in the world in a way they have not? Or, for that matter, imagine partners or spouses, who over the years, have drifted apart. What do they have to offer one another?

Feeling that we have nothing to say shouldn't stop us from writing a forever letter. Each of us has something unique to offer to the children, parents, spouse, or friends to whom we're writing. It's up to us to figure out what that something is.

"I've Lived My Values. My Family Knows Who I Am."

My friend Amy asked her father to write her a forever letter. He was in his early sixties at the time. His excuse for not writing: "If you don't know who I am by now, either you're a fool or I'm a fraud." He never did write one. To this day, Amy wishes he had. He died at sixty-nine, and she often finds herself yearning to hear his voice.

"Let me tell you why I don't have to write a forever letter," many people say to me, so often it has become a refrain. "My family knows who I am. My family knows what I stand for. My family knows how I feel about them. If they don't, I haven't been successful."

We understand this line of thought. We communicate our values by the way we live our lives, by our actions and our words, by the books and objects we collect and treasure.

To write a letter stating what we believe when we have lived our beliefs seems unnecessary, even redundant. Don't our lives speak loud enough? We're even taught that our actions speak louder than our words. If this is true, what more can the written word add?

A lot, I say.

The written word preserves the spoken word, and the written word preserves our actions.

By writing down what matters to us and by explaining how what matters to us motivates us to live the way we live, we enable our actions to live on long after we do. Imagine some years after we die, a child being named in our memory. Stories will undoubtedly be told about us. Photographs will be shown. But what will be left of our understanding of ourselves and of our actions? Imagine our namesake being able to read our words. Won't it make what we did and how we lived so much more real?

"I Want to Wait until the Person I'm Writing To Is Older."

"I'm thinking of writing to my son, but he's only six. I want to wait a few years. I want to write to him when he's older, when I have more of a sense of who he's on the road to becoming." It makes sense, doesn't it? To wait a few years until a child is more fully formed to know what we want to highlight, what we sense that child might need to hear? But this, too, is an excuse.

It was my excuse. I had been speaking around the country on forever letters for several years before someone asked me if I had written one to my son. In retrospect, I'm surprised I wasn't asked this question earlier. "No," I said, and I proceeded to deliver the above excuse. I believe that the person who asked was a man in his late sixties. I don't recall his face. All I recall are his eyes, eyes that bored a hole right through my being. He waited a few moments before he said, "Don't you think you should?" Another moment of silence. "After all, you're asking us to do it."

Busted.

That's how I came to write to Gabriel. He may have been too young to read it then, but I knew that one day, at some later point in his life, he would. Even more than this, writing to Gabriel was something I needed to do for me: to clarify my values, to determine how I was failing and succeeding as his mother, and to enable me to figure out how to change for the better. Even teachers need teachers. To this teacher, whose face and name I no longer recall, I remain grateful.

We will always have more to say to the youth in our lives as they age and as our relationships with them develop and mature. It goes without saying that what we write to them when they're toddlers will be different than what we write to them when they come of age, go off to college, get their first jobs, or when they're about to be married or have their first child. To address their growth and our ever-changing relationship, we can, at some later point in time, either add on to a forever letter we've already written to them or write them an additional one; but we must begin somewhere. Why miss the opportunity?

"I WANT TO WAIT UNTIL I'M OLDER."

If I write now, while I'm still young, say, in my twenties, thirties, forties, even fifties, I won't have said all I want to say. I'm not even sure of all I want to say. I have a lot more living to do. I keep on learning. I must wait. I don't want to leave anything out.

This is true. But just as our youth need different guidance at different life stages, we have different guidance to offer them based on the life stages we're in and the struggles and challenges we face: as a young widowed mother, a father who entered a new career, an aunt who had a child with in vitro because she was getting older and didn't want to make her motherhood dependent on meeting the man of her dreams, a mentor deciding to enlist, a boss leaving his job at a major manufacturing firm to become a teacher.

We're always in process. We're like a symphony being composed, a poem being crafted, a canvas being painted, a book being written. We continue to grow. We continue to change. We continue to need the inner process of reflection and introspection that writing forever letters provides. And still, we are all whole people at each point in our lives. It would be a shame if we thought our words mattered only when we reached a certain age. We must write a forever letter now, and if we feel the need to add more or write another at a later point in time, we can.

"I'LL GET TO IT EVENTUALLY."

We're busy. Busy studying, socializing, texting, earning a living, building a business, traveling, buying groceries, doing laundry, raising children, attending teacher conferences, caring for aging parents, exercising, reading, volunteering, serving on boards of organizations, mentoring younger professionals in our fields, spending time with family and friends, baby-sitting our grandchildren, going to doctors.

Or we're perpetual procrastinators. "I'll get to it," we say but rarely do.

My friend Amy also asked her mother to write her a forever letter. Her mother's response, "I'll get to it eventually." Amy knew her mother well enough to know that the "eventually" about which her mother spoke would never arrive.

Alice, the principal of an elementary school, understood herself well enough to know that she would achieve greater success in her position if she had a coach to help her get a handle on her day-to-day challenges. She had money in her budget to make it happen, but she barely had enough time to tackle her day-to-day challenges; so, she put off searching for a coach. Alice knew this was a mistake, but she made the decision that finding a coach was not her top priority, at least not at that moment, and I don't think she ever made it her top priority.

We all do this. We do what we have to do, and we put off what we can put off. What takes the back seat is often what we find most meaningful, balancing, or enlivening. How many of us refuse to study abroad in high school because we're afraid that we won't get into a good college, but know that what we most want is to learn a new language and immerse ourselves in a different culture? How many of us refuse to take time off from work because we're so busy, and yet we know that, if we don't, the loss of our soul is at stake? How many of us feel we must say yes to every walk, dinner, celebration, or fundraising event because we must show our faces, and yet we're aware that every extra commitment we take on is yet more time away from our friends, family, or from ourselves? How many of us fail to spend time with our aging parents because we're too busy raising our children, but when we finally make time, our parents no longer know who we are?

There is a voice inside each of us begging us to take better care of ourselves, begging us to make ourselves and the fulfillment of our values a priority. Writing a forever letter is a way of listening to that voice.

"I'm Afraid I'll Say Something Damaging."

Some of us might be afraid that our forever letter will do more damage than good. Situations in which this may be the case: writing to people who are fragile emotionally, who have psychological problems, who are not self-aware, who live in heightened states of anxiety, or to whom we feel we have nothing positive or loving to say.

If you're considering writing to someone whom you think will be unable to understand your words or the intention of your words because of their lack of emotional or cognitive abilities, you may want to think twice about writing to this person; but before you give up, turn to chapter 5 to see how you can write in a way that even these individuals might be able to understand. If after reading chapter 5 you come to the same conclusion, trust your instincts. Should you decide to give it a go, focus on this: you have an opportunity to say something positive, to find the good in the person you're writing to; and maybe, if you do, your words can help that person grow his or her self-esteem.

Rabbi Nachman of Bratslav, the great-grandson of the Baal Shem Tov, the founder of Hasidism, advises us not to give up on others. He encourages us to find the good in another human being, because by locating that good (even when it is hard to find), and by acknowledging it, we may be able to help that person find the good in him- or herself, and can perhaps even encourage that person to change his or her life for the better. He also understands that, if we have trouble finding the good in others, we may have trouble finding the good in ourselves, and that, if we judge others harshly, we're capable of judging ourselves harshly, too; so, just as he advises us not to give up on others, he advises us not to give up on ourselves, and encourages us to dig deep within to find our own good. [26]

When we write a forever letter, we can refrain from doing damage to another by finding in that other his or her good, and when we find that person's good, perhaps we will be motivated to find our own good, too.

"I Don't Want to Think about Death. I'm Still Young. I Have Plenty of Time."

People often say to me, "I'll write my forever letter someday but not now, not yet. I'm still young. I have plenty of time."

If you think that most people who offer this excuse are in their twenties, thirties, forties, even fifties, you're right; but a fair number are in their sixties and seventies. These folks often continue, "I know I'm older, but I'm fit. The doctor says I'm in good shape. I have nothing to worry about."

Here's what I say to all, no matter how young: Writing a forever letter is not just about contemplating our lives at the end of our lives. It's about contemplating how we live our lives now. This we can do at any age. We never know how long we will live. We never know how long those we love will live. So why wait?

I understand that we don't want to think about our mortality and that, on the rare occasions we do, we think of our death as distant, impossible, illogical, and absurd—a horror film in which we refuse to star. After all, we're healthy. We do yoga, Pilates, and Feldenkrais. We swim. We run. We play pickup basketball two nights a week. We take daily walks. We meditate. We consume vitamins and minerals, fish oils and antioxidants. But these choices do not guarantee that we will live a long life, and we know it.

---

26 Arthur Green, *Ehyeh: A Kabbalah for Tomorrow* (Woodstock, VT: Jewish Lights Publishing, 2004), 127–130.

Most of us know people who have died from sudden heart attacks, who have been killed in car accidents, who have been diagnosed with MS or early onset Alzheimer's, who have died from brain tumors, breast cancer, pancreatic cancer, or AIDS. Some of us even know people who have been victims of terrorism.

In a writing workshop, Bill, sixty-two, told the group that, when he was fifty-two, his twenty-three-year-old daughter, Emily, sent him the children's book *Guess How Much I Love You* by Sam McBratney. Bill was particularly grateful for this gift, as, not long after Emily sent it, she died of a brain tumor.

Raheen Heighter loved to draw. He exhibited his artwork in local fairs. His dream: to graduate college and to go into business, but he couldn't afford college, so he signed up for the military, hoping to gain some experience and get financial aid. Heighter went to Korea for a year, and after returning home, was deployed to Iraq. In a letter to his mother written from Iraq, he thanked her for being there for him, for recognizing his talents and gifts, and for, essentially, caring for his soul. [27] Not long thereafter his convoy was ambushed north of Baghdad. He was killed at the age of twenty-two.

As I was writing this book, David, a close family friend, went on a day hike in the Washington Cascades. He made it to the top, where he was able to witness the spectacular view of Mt. Stuart and the Enchantments. Then he collapsed. Two of his fellow hikers, both doctors, tried to revive him, but they couldn't. David was fifty-six, and, as far as anyone knew, in good health. The news of his death was a shock to everyone. "No, you can't mean *David!*" "You're kidding me, right?" "What? Impossible! I just saw him a few days ago." Here was a healthy man who was so vital, alive, and full of life, now dead. It was hard to believe.

---

27 *Last Letters Home: Voices of Americans from the Battlefields of Iraq* (New York: Life Books, 2004), 88. Also directed by Bill Couturie (HBO Studios; 2005), DVD.

In April 2012, I helped my seventy-four-year-old father organize his bookshelves. It was his request, partly to pass on some of his books and partly to clear out clutter. "Whatever you want, take," he said. My incentive was less the books he wanted to pass on and more the desire to help him downsize. I began with his bedroom bookshelf. I took out all the books, and I asked him to decide whether he wanted them or not. We made piles: books for him to keep, books for me, for other family members, for friends.

I wiped down the bookshelves, organized the books by category—fiction, nonfiction, poetry—set books by the same author side by side, and began the process of returning the books to the shelves. Several times during this process my father had to pause. It was exhausting physically and emotionally. I continued to work though his breaks. Five hours later, we were done. Initially, my father was thrilled. The organization delighted him. He kept walking into his bedroom to witness the transformation, but after his initial delight, the organized bookshelves unnerved him. "I know it's silly," he said to me, "but a friend told me years ago that the reason I never got my books in order was because I thought that, when I did, all my work would be done and I would have no more reason to live. I know it's crazy, but I'm on edge."

My father is not a superstitious man. Yet, organizing his bookshelves somehow felt like an invitation to the Angel of Death. Take note, O Angel of Death. Everything's done. I'm ready. Come posthaste.

We avoid activities that cause us to contemplate our death, but we must understand that when we contemplate our death, we are actually contemplating our life. We live more fully when we realize we will not live forever. Psychiatrist Elisabeth Kübler-Ross put it this way:

> It is the denial of death that is partially responsible for people
> living empty, purposeless lives; for when you live as if you'll live
> forever, it becomes too easy to postpone the things you know

that you must do. You live your life in preparation for tomorrow or in remembrance of yesterday, and meanwhile, each day is lost. In contrast, when you fully understand that each day you awaken could be the last you have, you take the time *that day* to grow, to become more of who you really are, to reach out to other human beings. [28]

To say that we don't want to write a forever letter because we don't want to think about death robs us of our ability to live a more nearly complete life. If we wait to write until we're able to sense death's approach, we might be racked with pain, consumed with anger, devastated by depression, or too busy saying goodbye to the people we love to have the wherewithal or the desire. Better to write when we're healthy, have our wits about us, and can think clearly.

My father was thirty-eight when he wrote his forever letter to us, his four children who were between the ages of nine and fourteen. I imagine that, when he sat down to write, he never considered the possibility that three years later his youngest son, Rafi, would die of Ewing's sarcoma.

We don't know when we will die. We don't know when the people we love will die. It's important that we share how we feel while we still can.

---

28   Elisabeth Kübler-Ross, *Death: The Final Stage of Growth* (New York: Simon & Schuster, 1975), 164.

4

WHAT MATTERS MOST?

How we spend our days is, of course, how we spend our lives.
—ANNIE DILLARD [29]

In this chapter, I highlight some of the values that matter to me. I could have easily chosen others, such as: be patient, maintain a work-life balance, take risks, enjoy solitude, trust your gut, fail your way into success, hold onto humor, play. The list is endless. My purpose in highlighting some of the values that matter to me is to encourage you to think about what matters to you.

LIVE YOUR TRUTH

To live a life true to ourselves, we must know who we are and what we stand for, and we must know what gives us joy and purpose. This is what

---

29   Annie Dillard, *The Writing Life* (New York: Harper & Row, 1989), 32.

Shakespeare meant when he wrote in *Hamlet*, "To thine own self be true." [30]
This is what the theologian Howard Thurman meant when he wrote, "Don't ask what the world needs. Ask what makes you come alive, and go do it. Because what the world needs is people who have come alive." [31]

This is what the cultural anthropologist Ernest Becker meant when he wrote,

> This, after all is said and done, is the only real problem of life, the only worthwhile preoccupation of man: What is one's true talent, his secret gift, his authentic vocation? In what way is one truly unique, and how can he express this uniqueness, give it form, dedicate it to something beyond himself? How can the person take his private inner being, the great mystery that he feels at the heart of himself, his emotions, his yearnings and use them to live more distinctively, to enrich both himself and mankind with the peculiar quality of his talent? [32]

This call to live our truth, or as C. G. Jung would have said, to live our "authentic selves," is unique to each of us; and for many of us this call changes throughout the course of our lives. While what calls to me now, in my mid-fifties, is similar to what called to me in my thirties—spending time with family and friends, writing, counseling, speaking, teaching, walking, and swimming—I find myself prioritizing these activities differently. I also find myself delighting more in my solitude, in playing with young children, and in holding sacred the time I spend with my parents, not knowing how many more years we'll have together.

---

30 William Shakespeare, *Hamlet* in *The Oxford Shakespeare*, ed. W. J. Craig (London: Oxford University Press, 1914), act 1, sc. 3, line 85.

31 Howard Thurman qtd. in Gil Bailie, *Violence Unveiled: Humanity at the Crossroads* (New York: Crossroad, 1995), xv.

32 Ernest Becker, *The Denial of Death* (New York: Free Press, 1997), 82.

In her book *Necessary Losses: The Loves, Illusions, Dependencies, and Impossible Expectations That All of Us Have to Give Up in Order to Grow*, Judith Viorst, psychoanalysis researcher, acknowledges the shifting images of ourselves in our middle years when she writes,

> We will mourn the loss of others. But we are also going to mourn
> the loss of our selves—of earlier definitions that our images of self
> depend upon. For the changes in our body redefine us. The events
> of our personal history redefine us. The ways that others perceive
> us redefine us. And at several points in our life we will have to
> relinquish a former self-image and move on. [33]

As my body acquires more aches and pains, as I look in the mirror and see that my salt-and-pepper hair seems to be more salt than pepper, as I find myself less interested in "making it" in a specific job or position and less interested in taking on "asks" to please others, as I struggle to listen to my authentic self and to begin to feel "I'm good enough," as I try to keep up with my former thirty-year-old self and realize I can't, I understand that my expectations of myself must change so that I may live my life without being disappointed in myself every step of the way.

In this middle period of my life, as my mortality comes into sharper focus, I feel a shift in my sense of time. On the one hand, I feel a greater sense of urgency. The question of what I want to accomplish in my life is no longer remote but near. On the other hand, I observe in myself a desire to slow down: to savor the sounds of laughter, the crash of thunder, the smell of burning wood, the taste of an apricot, and the way the winter light falls on a particular pine tree. The following words, believed to be attributed to poet and writer Diane Ackerman resonate for me: "I don't

---

33   Judith Viorst, *Necessary Losses: The Loves, Illusions, Dependencies, and Impossible
     Expectations That All of Us Have to Give Up in Order to Grow* (New York: Fawcett Gold
     Medal, 1987), 296.

want to get to the end of my life and find that I have lived just the length of it. I want to have lived the width of it as well."[34]

When we don't live the width of our lives, our unconscious knows, and our unconscious lets our bodies know, and our bodies let us know. In this regard, the mind-body connection is incredibly powerful. There have been a few times in my life when I thought I was living true to myself, true to what I claimed I wanted to be doing in this world, but my body let me know that I was not. I remember one time in particular when I created a rabbinic position for myself with a Jewish organization that claimed they wanted to make Judaism a greater part of their mission. After working in this organization for a couple months, I understood that this simply wasn't true and I was fighting an uphill battle. I wasn't aware of the toll this was taking on me until I listened to my body and realized that I had an infection for most of the time I worked at this organization. To this day I remember this infection as a sign that I wasn't living my truth and that it was time for me to move on.

Psychic Sonia Choquette in her book *Trust Your Vibes: Secret Tools for Six-Sensory Living* has this to say about the mind-body connection:

> Not only is the body an honest six-sensory channel, it's also fairly straightforward. In other words, if you're on the right track doing what serves your soul, then you're going to feel good, relaxed, and peaceful. Your heart will beat steadily, your energy will remain high, and you'll be relatively free from aches, pains, anxiety, or stress. If, on the other hand, you're making poor choices that compromise your spirit, or if you find yourself in circumstances that threaten or disrupt your psychic well-being, your body will communicate this as well.[35]

---

34   Diane Ackerman, attr.

35   Sonia Choquette, *Trust Your Vibes: Secret Tools for Six-Sensory Living* (Carlsbad, CA: Hay House, 2004), Kindle edition.

Choquette is not alone. There's been a great deal of research on the mind-body connection. Joan Borysenko,[36] Jon Kabat-Zinn,[37] and others have built their careers urging us to tend to this connection.

No matter how hard we try, there will undoubtedly be times in all of our lives when we struggle to live true to ourselves because we're afraid to hurt the people we love, or because we doubt our abilities to meet the challenges we've set for ourselves, or because we're trying to live into several truths that are at odds with each other, or because our image of who we are clashes with our image of who we want to be and the image of who we are suddenly isn't good enough, or because our image of who we are clashes with the image of who others want or need us to be.

Are you living your truth? Are you living your "authentic self"? When you write your forever letter, consider writing about your experiences over the years as you've tried to live your truth. Write about your successes and your failures. Do so not solely to share your experiences, but also to encourage the people you love to live their truth, sooner rather than later.

GIVE

It was March of 1980, three months before my brother Rafi died, though we had no idea at that time that death was on its way. The holiday of Passover was approaching. Rafi was lying in bed in a single room on the second floor of the pediatric oncology unit at Rhode Island Hospital, paralyzed from the waist down and undergoing chemo and radiation. One evening when my sister Sarina, my brother Ari, and I were at the hospital, Rafi, smiling and full of love, said that he had something he wanted to give us, and he handed each of us a box of our favorite Passover gum. That

---

36   Joan Borysenko, *Minding the Body, Mending the Mind* (Reading, MA: Addison-Wesley, 1987).

37   Jon Kabat-Zinn, *Full Catastrophe Living: Using the Wisdom of Your Body and Mind to Face Stress, Pain, and Illness* (New York: Delta Trade Paperbacks, 2009).

he thought about giving us a gift when he was in such a hard place made us feel so loved. We felt his love again later that evening when our mother told us the backstory. Rafi had not just sent Mom out to buy us the gum; he had asked her to go to the bank and withdraw money from his account in order to do so. He wanted the gum to be his gift. Rafi loved to give.

So does my husband. One day Seth was so excited to give me a gift he couldn't contain his enthusiasm. "I got you a present that you don't even know you need," he said. It wasn't my birthday. It wasn't our anniversary. There was no special occasion. It was a present just because. Seth kept me guessing for a while before he handed over a zipped black canvas case, not quite 8 inches wide by 11 inches long, with the word *Sennheiser* written on the front. I unzipped it to find a pair of large black headphones, and I looked at him with an expression that said, "What do I need this for?" He responded: "They're voice-cancelling headphones. You wear them on the plane, and you're supposed to arrive at your destination feeling more relaxed and refreshed. Since you're doing more traveling now with your speaking and workshops, I figured they would help you." He was right. Each time I wear them, I arrive at my destination refreshed, and I appreciate his gift anew.

Edith, a family friend now in her nineties, also loves to give. She's been on the giving end since I've known her: taking food to families in mourning, shopping for those unable to make it to the market. Though, as she ages, she is less able to give in the same ways, giving is part of the fabric of her being. Once, I asked her why. She said this: "I give because I want to, because I feel those of us who can, should. It's as simple as that." She then added, "I feel better about myself when I give."

I understand that feeling. I, too, feel better about myself when I give. One sunny summer day over eighteen years ago, shortly after I moved to Seattle, I took the day off, and I walked around Fremont and Queen Anne checking out the neighborhoods and the shops to get a feel for this new place I was calling home. On Queen Anne Avenue, I walked into an ice cream shop. The proprietor took one look at the sweater I was wearing (a lavender cotton button-down) and said she loved the color. I took off my sweater, and I handed it to her saying, "You should have this sweater. You like it so much." At first she declined, but I insisted. She wanted to return the favor by giving me an ice cream cone. It was still too early in the day for ice cream, but I assured her that I'd return and take her up on it. I don't believe I ever did. I moved to a different neighborhood, had a child, life got busy. I'm convinced that the only reason I remember this day, when so many other days of walking around neighborhoods I no longer recall, is because I gave this woman my sweater, and doing so made me feel alive in a different way. I continue to take off sweaters, necklaces, and bracelets and hand them to people who like them. Not all the time; sometimes I do hold onto my things, but the delight I get in giving items away often exceeds my enjoyment in wearing them.

When we think of giving gifts we often think of giving something concrete: a present, money, even a forever letter. But gifts can be intangible, too. Edith understood this. She not only gave to people in our community in concrete ways by delivering food, she also gave in intangible ways, like taking people to doctors' appointments (a gift of which I was a recipient), driving to visit friends of hers who were no longer driving, and now that she is no longer driving, reaching out to friends nearby whose mental capacities are waning.

As I think of the many intangible gifts I have received, I'm reminded of a gift I received not all that long ago from a five-year-old boy in a Montessori kindergarten class. Having mentioned to my friend, the school's director, that I was feeling out of sorts and depleted, and I sensed that what my soul needed was to be around children, to experience their joy and their sense of possibility, she invited me to her school for a visit. As I walked around the classroom, one child called me over to look at his painting, another to look at her drawing, and another to look at her book.

About twenty minutes after I arrived, the director invited me to participate in circle time, where we sang songs and where she introduced me as a friend whose son, Gabriel, had attended this school a long time ago. She said a few words about Gabriel and then asked me to show everyone a photograph of him, so I took out my cell phone, found his photo, and passed my phone around. I was so happy to be a part of this circle and felt so much love for the children in the room.

As parents started to arrive to pick up their children and the circle got smaller, one of the older boys shimmied over to me on his knees, sidled up to me, and said "I love you." Then with a sweep of his hand, signifying everyone else in the circle, he said, "We all love you." His words were a gift. They communicated to me that he felt the love I brought into the room, and that he sensed that everyone in the room felt the same way. His words also confirmed what I already knew, that my soul yearns to be around children.

In their happiness workshops, Rick Foster and Greg Hicks use an exercise called *musical chairs* during which they rotate everyone in the group through two lines of chairs that face each other. Their instructions to the attendees: "Give each person in this room a gift." Foster and Hicks write that they initially get some resistance, that many people take their request literally and are unsure how to proceed, but that by the end of the workshop all present feel buoyed by giving to one another in these more intangible ways. [38] We can be in service any time we want and in any situation in which we find ourselves. When we truly give, be it gifts or our time, we stop thinking about ourselves and begin to focus on the other.

Do you find that giving represents a significant part of who you are or do you find yourself wanting to give more? When you write your forever letter, contemplate writing about the times in your life when you've

---

38   Rick Foster and Greg Hicks, *How We Choose to Be Happy: The 9 Choices of Extremely Happy People—Their Secrets, Their Stories* (New York: Perigee, 1999), 173–174.

given, and how giving has made you feel, and about the times in your life when you've withheld from giving, and how that has made you feel. Also consider writing about the gifts the person you're writing to has given you: gifts of goods, words, or the gift of just "being there," and how you felt upon receiving these gifts.

TAKE RESPONSIBILITY

Before President-elect Barack Obama was sworn in as the forty-fourth president of the United States, he wrote to his daughters, Malia and Sasha, explaining why he had run for president. In his letter, Obama highlighted his feelings of responsibility and expressed his hope that his daughters would one day come to feel that same sense of responsibility.

> I hope both of you will take up that work [the unfinished work
> of perfecting America], righting the wrongs that you see and
> working to give others the chances you've had. Not just because
> you have an obligation to give something back to this country
> that has given our family so much—although you do have that
> obligation. But because you have an obligation to yourself.
> Because it is only when you hitch your wagon to something
> larger than yourself that you will realize your true potential. [39]

Many women I've admired over the years took up issues larger than themselves to help right the wrongs in our society, and thereby realized their potential: Dorothea Dix advocated for the mentally ill and for the physically handicapped; Harriet Beecher Stowe, in her novel *Uncle Tom's Cabin*, galvanized the antislavery movement by calling attention to the savagery and barbarity of slavery; Harriet Tubman rescued about seventy slaves with the help of the Underground Railroad.

---

39 Barack Obama, "What I Want for You—and Every Child in America," *Parade Magazine*, January 2009, 5.

Elizabeth Cady Stanton, mother of seven, advocated for the rights of women from the mid-1800s to the early 1900s. In 1872, she wrote a letter to Madge, her twenty-year-old daughter who was then a student at Vassar, about her day-to-day work lecturing in different communities. She highlighted the importance of encouraging women to think and to develop self-respect and confidence. In the final sentences of her letter, she inspired Madge to take responsibility for herself: "Now, improve every hour and every opportunity, and fit yourself for a good teacher or professor, so that you can have money of your own and not be obliged to depend on any man for every breath you draw. The helpless dependence of women generally makes them the narrow, discontented beings so many are." [40]

Chip Ward also took up issues larger than himself to help right the wrongs in our society. Ward became a political activist and grassroots organizer over two decades ago when he noticed too many children suffering from serious illnesses and deaths due to fallout radiation from nuclear testing in Utah's high desert valley, where he lived. On March 20, 2012, he wrote a letter to his almost four-year-old granddaughter, Madeline, in which he took responsibility for the irresponsible environmental choices made by his generation, and he apologized on behalf of himself and his generation for the deleterious effects these choices—using up the oil, the fertile soil, the forests, and the oceans, and adding chemicals and carbon—had on the environment. In his words:

> There were plenty of signs we took a wrong turn but we
> kept on going. Dumb, stubborn, blind: Who knows why we
> couldn't stop? Greed maybe—powerful corporations we couldn't
> overcome. It won't matter much to you who is to blame. You'll

---

40   Elizabeth Cady Stanton to Margaret L. Stanton, December 1, 1872, from *Papers of Elizabeth Cady Stanton, 1814–1946,* Library of Congress, hdl.loc.gov/loc.mss /eadmss.ms998020. Also in Dorie McCullough Lawson, *Posterity: Letters of Great Americans to Their Children* (New York: Doubleday, 2004), 10.

be too busy coping in the diminished world we bequeath you ... I know a better world is possible. We create that better world by reaching out to one another, listening, learning, and speaking from our hearts, face to face, neighbor to neighbor, one community after another, openly, inclusively, bravely. [41]

Some years ago, in a writing workshop, Ralph, a dapper eighty-five-year-old, jotted off a four-paragraph forever letter to his children and grandchildren. He wrote, "You have heard me state many times the adage, 'Do not separate yourself from the Community.' [42] I can think of nothing that is more important. I have lived my life that way and the benefits that have flowed from that activity have made my life more worthwhile. I commend that to you, for you too will recognize the benefits therefrom."

When you write your forever letter, consider encouraging the people you love not to stand idly by and leave the hard work of repairing this world to others, but to add their voices and their actions to help this world become a better place.

NEVER STOP ASKING QUESTIONS

As a young adult, I heard a story about physicist and Nobel laureate Isidor Rabi, who was asked how he had become a scientist. He attributed his decision to his mother, who, every day upon his return home from school, would say, "Izzy, did you ask a good question today?" Rabi's mother's question not only challenged her son to ask questions but also gave the two of them something to discuss when he returned home from school.

---

41   Chip Ward, "A Letter of Apology to My Granddaughter," TomDispatch.com: A Regular Antidote to the Mainstream Media (blog) March 27, 2012, www .tomdispatch.com/post/175521/.

42   *Ethics of the Fathers*, trans. Elana Zaiman (private collection), 2:5.

Mac used a similar technique with his daughter, Tabatha. As a young father, Mac traveled a lot for business. When he called home, he noticed that Tabatha never wanted to stay on the phone and it made him sad. So, he came up with an idea. He'd ask her a question. One day he happened upon the magic question: "Did you laugh today?" That question got Tabatha talking about her day. From that moment on, whenever he called home to check in, that's the question he would ask.

Master teachers almost always use questions in their teaching. Unless they ask their students questions and unless they encourage their students to ask questions, how can they know if their students understand the material they have taught? This encouragement of critical thinking is known as the Socratic method, and it's all the rage these days with today's schools returning to inquiry-based education. Questions push us forward, expand our horizons, inspire us, challenge us, and encourage us to continue to search for answers.

In *Something Like an Autobiography*, filmmaker Akira Kurosawa writes admiringly about how his film teacher, Yama-san, used questions in his teaching: "That's the kind of person Yama-san was. Even if he didn't like the footage we brought him from second-unit shooting, he always included it. Then when the film was finished and released in the theatres, he'd take us to see it. He would point out what he had done and say, 'Wouldn't it have been better to do that this way?' and patiently explain why. His attitude was that in order to train his associate directors it was worth sacrificing his own pictures. At least, that seems to me the only possible interpretation."[43]

Rainer Maria Rilke, an early twentieth century Bohemian-Austrian poet and novelist, also believed in the power questions. In *Letters to a Young Poet*, Rilke advised Franz Xaver Kappus—a nineteen-year-old novice poet and student at the same military academy Rilke himself had once

---

43 Akira Kurosawa, *Something Like an Autobiography* (New York: Vintage Books, 1983), 100.

attended—on writing and life. He encouraged Kappus not only to question but to appreciate the process of questioning—to "love the questions" and to "live the questions"—because in doing so he would continue to learn, and to "live … into the answer." [44]

A different approach to asking questions is presented by Reverend John Ames, the protagonist in Marilynne Robinson's novel *Gilead*. Ames suggests that we grow into ourselves and into our relationships when we understand every interaction we have with another human being as a question. He writes, "When you encounter another person, when you have dealings with anyone at all, it is as if a question is being put to you." [45] This is a powerful exercise. Try it out next time you encounter someone. Ask yourself what is being asked of you in that moment? Is it patience, gentleness, compassion? Is it guidance, love, humility? Is it a chance to better understand the other or to see our weaknesses and strengths mirrored to us by the other?

Here's one last approach to asking questions. It's offered by Ben Zoma in *Ethics of the Fathers*. [46] Ben Zoma asks and answers these four questions: Who is wise? Who is strong? Who is rich? And who is honored? Take a few moments to contemplate your answers to each of these questions before reading on.

Most of us assume that the answer to "Who is wise?" is someone who is smart; that the answer to "Who is strong?" is someone who possesses physical strength; that the answer to "Who is rich?" is someone who has amassed a fortune; and that the answer to "Who is honored?" is someone who has reached a certain status in the community based on wisdom or wealth.

These are not Ben Zoma's answers. Ben Zoma's answer to "Who is wise?" is "one who learns from all people." His answer to "Who is strong?"

---

44 Rainer Maria Rilke, *Letters to a Young Poet,* Letter Four, trans. Stephen Mitchell (New York: Random House, 1986), 34–35.

45 Marilynne Robinson, *Gilead* (New York: Farrar, Straus, Giroux, 2004), 124.

46 *Ethics of the Fathers*, trans. Elana Zaiman (private collection), 4:1.

is "one who is able to conquer his evil impulse." His answer to "Who is rich?" is "one who is happy with his lot." And his answer to "Who is honored?" is "one who honors his fellow creatures." The power of Ben Zoma's questions: they challenge our assumptions.

When you write your forever letter, consider writing about the importance of asking questions and being patient in search of the answers. Consider mentioning the technique that we see our encounters with others as questions. Consider asking questions of the people you love that challenge their assumptions and that encourage them to take an active role in learning something new about how they see themselves or how they perceive the world.

BE POSITIVE

In 2008 Maya Angelou published *Letter to My Daughter* to impart her wisdom and guidance. Angelou had no daughter. She wrote for daughters everywhere, for women of all ages, colors, and faiths. In her introduction, she champions a positive outlook:

> You may not control all the events that happen to you, but you can decide not to be reduced by them. Try to be a rainbow in someone's cloud. Do not complain. Make every effort to change things you do not like. If you cannot make a change, change the way you have been thinking. You might find a new solution. [47]

In a forever letter to his family, Dave, sixty-three, also wrote about the importance of adopting a positive attitude:

> You will be amazed how much a positive, optimistic attitude can mean in your life.

---

[47] Maya Angelou, *Letter to My Daughter* (New York: Random House, 2008), xii.

The possibilities of finding something negative to think about are endless. Too many people allow themselves to dwell on the negative: Seeing the glass as always half empty and forgetting that it is also half full.

Over my lifetime, I have come to understand that by being optimistic, one can change the outcome of events and achieve a far higher level of happiness at the same time.

This positive philosophy doesn't come automatically—it takes some work. But once you condition yourself to adopt a positive outlook—every day—it becomes a way of life.

We know this to be true. We know that when we're in a negative place, we not only bring ourselves down but we bring others down with us and that, when we're in a positive place, we lift ourselves up and we lift others up with us. We also know what it's like to be on the receiving end of someone else's attitude, that it's hard to be around people whose negative energy seems to seep out of their pores and to infect those around them, and that it's easy to be around people who are positive, as their energy uplifts those in their presence.

Years ago, I met Stanley, who, in his nineties, had such a negative attitude toward the world, his family, and his life, that many people found him hard to be around, myself included. Despite his negativity, I liked him. I found him bright and interesting. When we spent time together, Stanley would often complain about his health problems (which were real), his hard life, and his family, whom he felt were never as present to him as they could be. Frequently when he spoke, his voice was angry, and I found myself wondering on more than one occasion whether his family had made a deliberate choice to have as little to do with him as possible.

One day I realized that the time I spent with Stanley had begun to take a physical toll on me. His anger and negativity had worked their way into my body and left me depleted, yet another example of the mind-body connection. So I made a conscious decision to spend less time with him, to meet him on days when I had a lot of energy, to use humor, and to sandwich our visits between meetings that replenished. I also developed a self-protection imagery plan. Before I visited him, I imagined myself under a large, plastic, oval-shaped cover, and I carried this image with me into our visit. When Stanley spouted his anger and negativity, I visualized his words hitting the plastic cover that surrounded me, bouncing off that cover, and evaporating into the air. This technique wasn't foolproof, but I fared better than I had before, and I came to this conclusion: If Stanley needed his negative energy to survive, that was his choice. I, too, had a choice. I didn't have to take his negative energy into my body.

Contrast Stanley with Rachel, in her eighties, who had once been a beloved teacher. Despite her dementia, Rachel was a woman in whose presence I felt uplifted. One day, as Rachel and I were talking about her life, I noticed on the seat of her walker a hardcover novel bookmarked near the book's end. "Are you enjoying your book?" I asked her. "Yes," she said. "It's a great book." When I asked her what it was about, she began to laugh. Her laughter was so contagious that I began to laugh with her, not quite sure why we were laughing.

When Rachel stopped laughing long enough to speak, she said, "I can't remember what it's about." Then she began to laugh again, and again I laughed with her. When we both stopped laughing, I said, "I'm amazed you can laugh at yourself. If I forgot the book I was reading, I think I'd be angry with myself." Her response I'll never forget. "There's nothing I can do about it, so why be angry?" If I make it to the time in my life when forgetfulness is my new normal, I hope that like Rachel, I, too, will be able to be positive about my memory loss.

In her book *Positivity*, researcher Barbara Fredrickson maintains that when we're positive, not only does our psychological health improve, but so does our resilience to face all that lies before us. [48]

Consider writing about positivity in your forever letter. Provide examples of positivity from your life experience or from the life experience of the persons you're writing to. Write about the way you work with your own attitude and the techniques you use to become more positive. If you have a hard time living positively, acknowledge that you're not always as successful as you'd like but that you continue to try.

Say, "I Believe in You."

It was the summer of 1980. I was seventeen and a CIT (counselor-in-training) for a group of eleven-year-old girls at an overnight camp I had not attended as a camper. They were a great group of girls, but it was a hard summer. I arrived at camp a week after Rafi had died with mixed feelings about being in a new place with people I did not know, being responsible for a bunk of girls, and feeling anxious about starting college, which would begin only a few days after camp would end. It's not that I didn't think I could handle it all, but after Rafi's death, I felt so raw, sad, and lost that I didn't have the confidence in myself to believe I could do it with grace.

My mom, who was grieving herself, came to the rescue. She wrote a letter to me at camp, where she expressed her belief in me with these words:

> Next Sunday [visiting day] we see you! That's really
> exciting. The more I reflect on GW [George Washington
> University], the more I'm delighted with your choice!
> Think of it like a new pair of shoes that need breaking in.
> After the initial getting used to … they're part of you. So,
> too … college … friends … schoolwork … play … Washington

---

48   Barbara Fredrickson, *Positivity* (New York: Crown, 2009), 9–13.

itself ... being on your own ... etc. You need only look at your
past to know NEW situations are hard. But with each one you've
blossomed even more ... and so you shall continue. [49]

Just as my mother's belief in me helped me to believe in myself, so
Laurie's belief in her daughter, Rebecca, helped Rebecca believe in herself.
Laurie, in her mid-fifties, gave me a lift to the airport after I had spent a
weekend in her community teaching about forever letters. In the car we
talked about Rebecca, then twenty-something, who had just moved home
again. I had gotten to know Rebecca. It was Rebecca who had picked me
up at the airport when I arrived, taken me to lunch, and attended the
weekend lectures and workshops alongside her mother. For both mother
and daughter, Rebecca's return home was an adjustment.

As Laurie looked out the driver's window and navigated the road to the
airport, she said, "Just as we were beginning to enjoy life without our children but given the economy, [50] it's hard for her to find steady work. I know
she's having a hard time. I believe in her. I know she'll find something."

"Tell her you believe in her," I said. "Tell her you admire her. Tell her
you're proud of her. Acknowledge the values that she's living. Write to her.
It will mean the world to her."

"I did," Laurie responded. "I wrote to her during the workshop this
morning." This was the workshop from which we had just come, the
workshop during which Laurie and Rebecca had sat side by side.

A few days later Laurie sent me this e-mail:

I was going to reread and edit the letter before I gave it to her,
but Monday night I picked her up at work and we stopped for a

---

49 Like my father, my mother also uses a series of periods that look like ellipses in
her writing. Again, in this excerpt, they are a stylistic feature and do not indicate
deletions of text. Material in brackets are my explanations.

50 Laurie is speaking of the recession in the first decade of the twenty-first century.

glass of wine and some quality time to chat. We had both been on different schedules and needed to do some catching up. It was very good for us. When we got home I just thought it was a good moment so gave it to her, explaining all that. She took it in the other room to read while I started dinner. She stayed away about twenty minutes to absorb it (I am sure it only took five minutes to read) and then came back in with tears in her eyes and gave me a big hug. She just said, "Thank you, I really needed to hear that."

We need to hear from our parents that they believe in us. We need to hear from other adults in our family and in our lives—teachers, mentors, grandparents, aunts, and uncles—that they also believe in us.

I can only imagine how James Baldwin's fifteen-year-old nephew, namesake, and godson must have felt when he read the words below from a letter his uncle wrote to him on the hundredth anniversary of the Emancipation:

> Wherever you have turned, James, in your short time on this earth, you have been told where you could go and what you could do (and *how* you could do it) and where you could live and whom you could marry. I know your countrymen do not agree with me about this, and I hear them saying, "You exaggerate." They do not know Harlem, and I do. So do you. Take no one's word for anything, including mine—but trust your experience. Know whence you came. If you know whence you came, there is really no limit to where you can go . . . .
>
> It will be hard, James, but you come from sturdy, peasant stock, men who picked cotton and dammed rivers and built railroads, and, in the teeth of the most terrifying odds, achieved an unassailable and monumental dignity. [51]

---

51 James Baldwin, "My Dungeon Shook," in *Collected Essays*, ed. Toni Morrison (New York: The Library of America, 1998), 293–294.

To believe in his nephew, to give his nephew the confidence to believe in himself as an African-American, and to put that belief in writing was a gift that his nephew could return to over and over whenever he felt his belief in himself as an African-American man beginning to wane.

It's clear that we need to hear from our elders that they believe in us. They've lived more years, had more experiences, and possess a knowledge of life that can help to guide us forward. It's also important to hear from our spouses and friends, our students and children, our cousins and siblings that they, too, believe in us. Their belief in us offers us a different kind of strength.

During a writing workshop for a small group of women, Ivy, a woman in her mid-fifties, cried as she told us about her decision, a few years prior, to leave a job that she hated because of all the politics and bureaucracy. One night, while she was still working at this job, she was sitting in her family room with a few close friends when she found herself in tears because of how unhappy she was in her job. Her twenty-something daughter happened to be home at the time, and when she saw her mom in tears, she decided to write her mom a letter. In this letter, she told her mom how much she believed in her. Ivy said that it was her daughter who gave her the strength to begin to make the changes she needed to leave that job and to move forward.

When I was in the middle of writing this book and doubting myself as a writer and a mother, because my book was taking so much of my time, Gabriel, then twelve years old, wrote me this letter, which on occasion I still pull out to read: "Mom, You are wonderful, caring, loving, sensitive, responsible, amazing, beautiful, and many more. If I were to write more it would take up the whole page and it would be too long. But when I see you nothing can be too long even your book. So go get the future and write your book so that there can be many more pages than just one. I love you."

My sister Sarina also believes in me as a writer. She has ever since we were young and I told her that I wanted to write. I'm grateful for her support all these years, especially during the times when I did not believe in myself.

We've all gone through hard times. We all know what it means not to believe in ourselves. We also know how important, even life-saving it is, to have others believe in us when we have difficulty believing in ourselves.

When you write a forever letter to people you love, tell them why you believe in them. Share with them a trying time in your life when you felt buoyed by another, and how that person's faith in you gave you the strength you needed to move forward. If you write to the people you love while they're in the midst of a trying time, perhaps your words will encourage them to believe themselves into brighter times.

LOVE

In a writing workshop, Josie, in her fifties, spoke about the last letter she and her sister received from their mother. In this letter their mother wrote about her life and her thoughts on mothering. She told her daughters that, though money and valuables would be part of their inheritance, the greatest inheritance they had already received, and that was love.

This was true for Jeff. In the excerpt below from the forever letter he wrote to his mother, Abby, when he was fourteen and in ninth grade, Jeff wrote about how much her love meant to him. The "bad times" Jeff refers to in his letter pertain to the time beginning two years after his parents' divorce when his brother got into alcohol and drugs, and his mom was laid off from her job and became depressed and depleted financially and emotionally:

> You have brought me up to be an excellent, well-mannered
> (most of the time) child. You have taught me to believe in
> myself, and I have. You showed me I *can* do things when I
> thought I could not. You told me you have faith in me. You told
> me over and over that you love me. We have been through hard
> times and easy times, old relationships and new ones, happy
> times and sad times, and through all the bad stuff, we have
> managed to get through them. Through the bad times when I

thought things could not get any better, you stayed positive and told me that "We'll get through this, I promise." You kept that promise and things would get better. I admire your strength, when you stayed strong when things seemed hopeless...

Through the good and bad times, I have loved you; and I will always love you.

When I asked Jeff's permission to include his forever letter in this book, I asked if he would put me in touch with his mom so I could ask her about her experience of receiving his letter. Abby and I spoke. She told me how much Jeff's letter meant to her. She said that she cried when she received it and tacked it up on her refrigerator, where it hangs to this day, though it has been through several moves and has yellowed over the years. She also said that she still carried some guilt about not having provided a stable home, but that when she and Jeff spoke (before he put her in touch with me), he assured her that he had always felt secure because she had always told him that everything would be okay, and he had no reason not to believe her.

Like Jeff, the one constant in Brenda's life when her parents' marriage dissolved (and uncertainty and chaos followed) was love. For Brenda, it was her grandmother's love. I learned about this love one day from a plum-colored spiral notebook sitting on her grandmother's coffee table which her grandmother pointed to with pride, saying, "See that book, it's from my granddaughter, Brenda, for my 100th birthday."

The first page featured two photographs: the first, a colored photograph of Brenda with her grandmother, cheeks touching and both smiling; the second, a black-and-white photograph of Brenda and her sister with their grandmother. The girls flank their grandmother, who is sandwiched between them, and their heads lean into hers. All three are smiling. Between these pictures in blue ink and in bold sixteen-inch typeface is the title of this slender volume, *A Lifetime of Love.*

This notebook contained five single-spaced typed pages that spoke to Brenda's relationship with her grandmother and about the love they shared over the years. In one place Brenda wrote, "The unconditional love I have been lucky enough to receive for fifty-five years has come almost entirely from this wonderful woman. In her eyes I am beautiful, thin, sweet, darling, and a genius. One has only to feel this love for a few minutes and the whole world can seem a much easier and wonderful place."

Brenda concluded by addressing her grandmother directly: "So, in case I haven't told you enough, you, my amazing, wonderful Grandma, have been the constant strength and love in my life and for that I am blessed and thankful. I love you more than words can say."

One final story about the power of love from my friend David, the healer. Years ago, when he was in massage school, his professor asked for a student to volunteer massage hours at a house for mentally and physically handicapped adults. David's initial response: fear. So he decided to confront his fear head on and offer his services.

One of his clients was Kim, twenty-three, with Down syndrome. When he first worked on Kim, he began by asking her to lie on her back. Though trained to begin a massage at the top of the body, he was so repulsed by Kim's face, he decided to begin at her arms.

When he asked Kim to turn over onto her stomach so that he could complete the massage, Kim became talkative. "You know why I'm here?" she asked. She didn't wait for David to respond. "I'm here because my mother doesn't love me." Hearing these words, David knew what he had to do. When he finished massaging Kim on her belly, he asked her to turn over again, and he finished the massage the way he should have begun. As he worked on her head and her face, Kim kept saying, "Ahh. Ahh. Ahh."

David returned to the house to offer more massages. On one of his visits, Kim showed up. At some point during her massage she asked David: "Did you notice that my fingernails and toenails are painted red?"

"Well, yes, I did," David said.

Her response, he'll never forget. "I did it for you."

Working with Kim, David came to a new understanding of love, an important lesson on his road to becoming a healer. This understanding of love is in keeping with the Hasidic Master Moshe Leib of Sassov's understanding of love. Rabbi Leib taught that to truly love someone means to know what causes that person pain. [52]

It's impossible in this short section to do justice to the topic of love, but contemplating the power of love reminds us how crucial love, in all its forms, is to our very being. We all need to be loved. Being loved gives us the courage to be ourselves and the confidence to tackle the tough stuff. Being loved enables us to love. In your forever letters consider telling the people you love *that* you love them, and *why* you love them. Let them know you're aware of what causes them pain, and even of what brings them joy. Communicate your love in whatever way you can so that they feel your love deep in the their bone marrow, and so that they understand the power of expressing their love to the people they love.

Show Compassion

Ada was born in 1916 in Feodosiya, Russia, a town on the Black Sea. She lived through the latter half of World War I and the whole of the Russian Revolution. At ninety-seven, she told me stories about her early childhood and about the compassionate people who saved her life and the lives of her family.

Growing up, Ada and her sister, Mathilda, never played outside because they were afraid of the Cossacks. When they heard the beating of horses' feet and Cossacks shouting, "Kill the Jews," Ada and her family would climb over the fence that separated their property from the property of the Polish woman who lived behind them, and run for shelter into this woman's home. This Polish woman took her life into her hands every time she hid them

---

52   Louis I. Newman, *The Hasidic Anthology: Tales and Teachings of the Hasidim* (Northvale, NJ: Jason Aronson, 1987), 221.

because, if the Cossacks discovered that she had sheltered Jews, both Ada and the Polish neighbor's family would have been killed.

Ada also told me about the baker, a Russian man, probably Greek Orthodox, who one day threw a loaf of bread onto their doorstep (for which they were grateful, as their food was rationed). A neighbor saw and ratted them out. Ada will never forget the terror she felt as the Cossacks ransacked their house and slashed open their feather beds in search of that loaf of bread. Had the Cossacks found it, they would have executed the baker, Ada, and her entire family, but they never found it. Ada's grandmother had hidden it deep in the ashes of their wall stove.

The word *compassion* is derived from the Latin *pati* and *cum*, which mean "to suffer with." To have compassion is to suffer with another. In Hebrew, the word for compassion is *rachamim*, from the Hebrew root, *reish-chet-mem*, pronounced *rechem*, meaning "womb." My friend and colleague Lia Bass speaks of the womb as a place that has the ability to both hold another within and to remain separate from that which it holds. A mother holds her child within, and yet mother and child are separate entities. To suffer with another, to hold another within, this is compassion.

We need to hear and to tell stories about compassion to remind us that we're all capable of compassion and that our simple acts of compassion go a long way. Compassion is not intellectual. Compassion happens when we let our hearts speak. The three stories that I offer below are stories, like Ada's story, about the compassion that happens when we let our hearts speak.

One day, years ago, as I was walking the halls in the nursing home where I served as a chaplain, I noticed Delores, a woman in her late eighties, sitting in her wheelchair outside her door knitting. "What are you making?" I asked. Delores said she was helping her next-door neighbor, Frema, who had been knitting a baby blanket for her soon-to-be-born grandchild. Delores realized that when Frema got sick there would be no way she would be able to finish knitting the blanket in time, so Delores let her heart speak by taking it upon herself to help.

In July 2013, on a family hike up to Delicate Arch in Moab, Utah, I witnessed many hearts speaking. Intrigued by a group of people headed down the mountain carrying a cardboard life-sized photograph of the head and shoulders of a clean-cut, handsome man in his late twenties, I stopped one of members of the group and asked, "Who's the person on the sign?" She said it was Todd, a friend of theirs who had been paralyzed for as long as she'd known him. "We're taking him with us on all of our hikes, and we're taking photographs with him. When we get home, we're going to print out our photographs and make an album of all the places he hiked with us." As I watched Todd's life-sized photograph wind further down the path, surrounded by his large group of his friends, I was in awe of their compassionate creativity.

Wiebke, an artist friend of mine, also discovered a way to let her heart speak through her compassionate creativity. It happened like this: Wiebke realized she was having trouble making time for her art, so she set a goal. She would create art on a postcard every day for an entire year, and she would mail these postcards to family and friends.

I was lucky to be the recipient of four postcards. The first, drawn in black ink and pencil, depicted a black bird sitting on a brown, leafless branch waiting to take flight. It arrived at the end of January 2012, the year I had taken my sabbatical to write this book. Seeing that bird alone on a branch, I recognized myself, sitting alone at my kitchen or dining room table, trying to commit words to the page. But as I stared at that postcard I realized that no bird would sit on a branch forever. Eventually that bird would take flight, and someday, so would my words.

When you write your forever letter to the people you love, consider writing about compassion. Share some of your acts of compassion. Tell stories about people who showed you compassion. Encourage the people you love to live with compassion. Appreciate them for the compassionate acts they already perform.

FOLLOW YOUR DREAMS

Langston Hughes, poet, playwright, novelist, and social activist, wrote a number of poems about the need to hold onto our dreams [53] and live into our dreams because he understood what happens to us when we don't. He understood that when we let go of our dreams, we lose our center and a piece of us dies. He understood that our dreams give us reason to live.

Computer Science Professor Randy Pausch understood the importance of dreams. Pausch lived his last days with pancreatic cancer that had metastasized to his liver. In his last lecture at Carnegie Mellon University, titled "Really Achieving Your Childhood Dreams," later published as *The Last Lecture*, he spoke about the importance of living into his dreams and being lucky enough to have had parents who encouraged him to do so. His childhood dreams: to be in zero gravity, play for the NFL, write an article for *World Book Encyclopedia*, be Captain Kirk, win stuffed animals, and be a Disney Imagineer. [54] Pausch didn't fulfill all of his dreams, but he did fulfill many, and he learned valuable lessons along the way.

Author Jodi Picoult also understands the importance of living into dreams. In "An Open Letter to My Oldest Son, as He Leaves for College," from *Leaving Home: Short Pieces*, Picoult encourages her son to live into his dreams by doing what he wants to do and not what he thinks he should do. She writes, "Remember me—with my one-in-a-million career path—the writer I hoped to be, instead of the teacher I assumed I'd be. Don't listen to people who ask you what on earth one does with a degree in Egyptology. If it's what you fall asleep thinking about, and wake up excited about, it's what you should pursue. The rest (including a paycheck) will somehow sort itself out." [55]

---

53   Langston Hughes, *The Collected Poems of Langston Hughes*, eds. Arnold Rampersad and David Roessel (New York: Alfred A. Knopf, 2007).

54   Randy Pausch, *The Last Lecture* (New York: Hyperion, 2008), 19.

55   Jodi Picoult, "An Open Letter to My Oldest Son, as He Leaves for College," *Leaving Home: Short Pieces* (Newton Highlands, MA: LGLA/Kindle Single, 2011).

Hughes', Pausch's, and Picoult's messages pertain to us. We must hold onto our dreams even when they feel far away or seem impractical. When I took a year off to fulfill my dream of writing this book, my friend Jonathan said to me, "You *know* you're *not* going to be able to write your book at home in your environment." I respect Jonathan, and I value our friendship; but I noticed that after his comment, I no longer discussed my book project with him. Though he voiced a concern nagging at me from within, his critical tone put me off. Had he approached me instead with more curiosity and less certainty—for example, had he asked, "Do you think you'll be able to write your book at home in your own environment?" or "Do you think you want to build in a few retreats during the year to give you the solitude you'll need to complete your project?"—I might have felt differently.

Now, in hindsight, I see that, while Jonathan's tone could have been more sensitive, my gut response probably had more to do with how I interpreted his comment than with how he may have intended for his comment to be understood. Had I been better able to acknowledge my fears, anxieties, and self-doubts as a natural part of the dream-creation process, perhaps I would not have shut him out and myself down.

This experience gave me a lot to think about. First, it made me understand that, when we voice our dreams, we must feel strong enough to stand by them, and even to enroll others in them. Second, we have to be careful how we respond to others who share their dreams with us. Had Jonathan been the one to tell me that he was going to write a book, I imagine I would have voiced a similar concern. I wonder if I would have had the wherewithal to choose my tone carefully and to ask him questions rather than to speak with certainty. Thinking this through made me realize that I have probably killed some dreams in my time, and not only my own. So came my challenge: How do I support the dreams of the people in my life? How do I take care not to impose my issues on them? How do I encourage them to move forward?

When you write your forever letter, consider encouraging the people you love to live into their dreams. Consider sharing some of your dreams—dreams you attained, dreams you tried to attain but were unable to reach, dreams you never attained because you never tried to live them—and some of the lessons you learned along the way.

EXPRESS GRATITUDE

Years ago, when I was in New England, I took a walk with Emma, my friend's five-year-old daughter. It was late October, autumn well under way. To get to know her better, I asked her questions. "What's your favorite dessert? Your favorite meal? Who's your favorite friend?" Her response to all my questions was that she had no favorites.

On we walked around her neighborhood, under large maples, oaks, and elms, breathing in cold air, stepping on leaves and grass. Hoping Emma would tell me more about her new doll, I asked her yet another question about favorites: "What's the most favorite thing in your room?"

Again she said that she had no favorites. While I was internally berating myself for asking her the "What's your favorite" question again, Emma paused. She said that she did have one favorite—being alive, because if she weren't alive she wouldn't get to see the leaves and the trees. She wouldn't get to see any of the beauty that surrounded her. Emma twirled herself around and around, delighted to be witness to a fall day in all its glory.

As I watched her twirl, as I felt her joy and gratitude, I remembered a similar twirl my son, Gabriel, did when he was two and a half. It was a late morning in mid-July. Seth, Gabriel, and I had driven with Seth's mom, Carol, and her husband, Larry, to a quiet section of the beach in west Seattle. It was Gabriel's first trip to the beach. There he stood with his blond curls and blue eyes, in his blue-and-magenta-striped outfit with a sagging diaper and a sturdy pair of blue shoes, taking it all in: the water, the sand, the crabs, the sea stars, the seaweed, the sun. Fully clothed, he walked into the shallow water of the receding wave, held his arms high up in the air, closed his eyes, and with a smile on his face began to turn around and around. The photograph that captures this moment sits in a magnetic frame on my file cabinet. Many photographs of Gabriel adorn this file cabinet; yet every time I see this photograph, I'm reminded of the human potential for gratitude.

Leah, whom I met when she was in her mid-eighties, had so much gratitude, I felt as if it were seeping out of her pores. Honest and insightful with a great sense of humor, and a terrific memory, Leah was a gem of a woman. She died at ninety-two, but not without writing a forever letter, excerpted below, in which she expressed her gratitude to her son and daughter-in-law in whose home she had lived for the last thirteen years of her life:

> Before Pa died, he told me what a wonderful home he had living with me. And he thanked me. And now I am writing to you to tell you how much I enjoyed living with you. And to thank you. For welcoming me into your home, and for taking such good care of me.

> Arlene, thank you for your daily doings of love. For bringing me orange juice on your way to work in the morning, and for bringing me a cup of tea and the paper in the evening. For washing my stockings without my even asking. For polishing my shoes. These little things meant so much to me.

> I am grateful to both of you for giving so much from your heart. And I am grateful to have had you both in my life.

Erin, a friend of mine, kept a gratitude journal on her bedside table, and each night before going to sleep, she wrote ten things that happened to her that day for which she was grateful. Inspired, I began a gratitude journal. I was surprised to discover how much trouble I had finding ten things each day for which I was grateful. Refusing to write the same list over and over again, I pushed myself to find new things. When I did, I realized there were many things I was grateful for that I was taking for granted. Things like: the kiss I got from Gabriel before he left for school, or the dinner Seth prepared, or the sunny day, or the phone call from a friend I hadn't heard from in a while. The more I pushed myself to find things for which I was grateful, the more grateful I became.

There are always things for which we can be grateful, even in the darkest of times, and it behooves us to find those things, because living with gratitude is so much healthier than drowning ourselves in sorrow. When you write a forever letter to the people you love, consider expressing your gratitude to them (be as specific as you can), and consider encouraging gratitude as a way of life.

LISTEN

My father-in-law told me about a friend of his whose wife often tells him that he's not hard of hearing but hard of listening. We're not always the best listeners. On occasion, we tune out. We tune out when we're tired, when listening is too painful, when we have other things on our minds, when we've heard someone tell the same story over and over, when we're wrapped up in our own personal dramas, or when we're multitasking. But we also know what it means to listen. When we're listening, really listening, our whole being is involved—our eyes, heart, and mind—and we not only feel present to the person we're listening to, but we feel present to ourselves.

As I was growing up, the person who most often modeled for Sarina, Ari, Rafi, and me what it meant to listen was our mother. On occasion, we took her listening for granted, assumed it was part of her job description as a mother, like making sandwiches for our lunches, being home when we returned from school, taking us to doctor appointments, dropping us off and picking us up from our friends' houses. Whenever we had news to share—a good grade, a positive encounter, a funny story—Mom was the one we would tell. It's not that we kept these things from our father, but he wasn't around as often, and when he was, we had the sense that he was less interested in the day-to-day, and that we could interrupt him only in an emergency.

In my childhood, we ate dinner together as a family most evenings. From these dinner conversations, I remember my father's voice. He always asked us lots of questions. My mother, on the other hand, was quiet unless she had something specific to add. I thought this was because my mother didn't feel comfortable inserting herself into the conversation when my father was on a roll, or that she wanted to offer her husband, the man of the house, respect. Perhaps this was part of her reasoning, but it took me until I was well into my adulthood to realize that my mother *had* inserted herself into the conversation, not as a talker, but as a listener.

Artist Anne Truitt has this to say about listening and motherhood: "The mother listens to her baby. She tunes her neural receivers to the baby's and then is able psychologically to hold her child, to prevent the child's feeling distress. This is the bliss of motherhood, this heavenly capacity to make another human being happy. This same attunement enables the mother to catch her baby's frustrations before they become too painful for the baby to accept." [56]

This total immersion, this oneness between mother and child, continues until the child begins to mature and to separate, but in my experience as a daughter (and later as a mother) there's something special about this kind of listening that continues on through the years. To this day, Sarina, Ari, and I still call our mother to tell her stories about ourselves, our spouses, our children, our work, our lives; it is she who shares our stories with our father, whose dislike of the phone and whose hearing loss make talking on it increasingly difficult.

As I think about my mother, I realize that like myself and most mothers I know, she was and remains engaged in the process of *tzimtzum*, contraction. This word comes from Lurianic Kabbalah's understanding of the

---

56   Anne Truitt, *Daybook: The Journal of an Artist* (New York: Penguin, 1984), 15.

creation of the world. Lurianic Kabbalah holds that the only way God could make space for the world to be created was to retract some of God's self from the world. Imagine God taking a deep breath in to make space for the creation of the world. Take a deep breath in. Feel the retraction. When we retract, when we pull our egos inward, we create space for others. This is true when we listen.

Mothers are not the only ones who know how to listen. Lots of people know how or learn how to listen. Therapists, coaches, doctors, clergy, teachers, and many others in the helping professions are trained to listen deeply to the voice, tone, gesture, words, silences, and heart of another.

There's a moving video on YouTube that speaks to the power of listening. Featured are Gladys Wilson and Naomi Feil, the founder of validation therapy. Gladys is an eighty-seven-year-old woman with Alzheimer's who's almost completely nonverbal. She's sitting in an aqua-green lounge chair wearing a violet sweater. Naomi is in her late seventies, with a full head of white hair, dressed in a maroon top. She approaches Gladys, leans into her, talks to her with soothing words, touches her shoulder, holds her hands, and in this way enters Gladys's world. Gladys responds. She reaches out for Naomi, and a tear falls from her eye. Naomi touches Gladys's cheeks with her fingertips and sings Gladys a church song about Jesus, adjusting her voice to the pace of Gladys's right hand tapping on the arm of her chair. When Naomi stops singing, Gladys pulls Naomi toward her. Their foreheads touch. Gladys opens her eyes and Naomi begins to sing again. This time she sings the chorus and the first stanza of "He's Got the Whole World in His Hands." When she returns to sing the chorus for the second time, the most miraculous thing happens: Gladys joins in. For a few moments the two of them sing together, and Gladys is transformed from being a prisoner in her own body to connecting with another human being.[57] She senses she is heard.

---

57   "Gladys Wilson and Naomi Feil," YouTube video, posted by Memorybridge, May 26, 2009, www.youtube.com/watch?v=CrZXz10FcVM.

One final story about listening: When I was fifty, I found it hard to sit for any length of time without crying. The pain began innocently enough with a pinch in my left hip that felt, every now and then when I put my left foot forward, as if my skin were seeping under my pelvic bone and getting stuck on it on the way out. The pain continued for months until an MRI of my hips revealed bilateral hip impingements and labral tears that led to two hip arthroscopies.

Pain changed me. I was not myself. I didn't know who I was. I became my pain. I said "my pain" and not "the pain," as if I willingly accepted this pain as a gift. I wanted to talk about other things, but my pain was all that seemed to matter. I feared I would never again be myself, that living in pain was my new normal. My mind took me places I didn't want to go.

A number of friends seemed to tire of hearing me talk about my pain, but a handful of friends checked in regularly, asked questions, and listened. I believe that their listening played an important role in helping me heal.

The good news is that listening is a learned skill. Listening can improve with intentional practice. When you write a forever letter to the people you love, consider writing about the importance of listening. Tell a story about a time you failed to listen with a full and open heart and how from this experience you learned how important it is to listen. Or, tell a story about a time you felt *really* listened to and the impact it had on both you and the person listening.

5

HOW TO INCREASE OUR CHANCES OF BEING HEARD

Only connect!
—E. M. FORSTER[58]

We never know how our words will affect another person; will that person understand our words in the way we intend our words to be understood? This fear stops many of us from writing. It shouldn't. It should, however, challenge us to be cognizant of how we show up in our writing. This chapter focuses on eight ways we can show up in our writing to increase our chances of being heard.

---

58   E. M. Forster, *Howards End* (New York: Alfred A Knopf, 1921), 214.

Be Present

When Gabriel was in elementary school, our weekday morning routine used to go something like this: My husband, Seth, would leave for work. I would wake up Gabriel at 7:15 a.m.; and while he passed through the fuzzy space between sleeping and waking, got out of bed, dressed, and brushed his teeth, I would shower, dress, and pack my bag for the day. We would then meet in the kitchen for a quick breakfast before he headed off to school and I headed off to work. On rushed weekday mornings we would eat dry cereal, but when time permitted, we would share a toasted bagel with cream cheese.

One Monday morning, after I had been out of town teaching for the weekend, our routine changed. When I entered the kitchen, Gabriel, then nine and a half, said, "Sit down, Mama. I made breakfast." I looked at the table. A cup of cold water and half a toasted bagel slathered with cream cheese sat at Gabriel's place. A mug of warm water and half a toasted bagel with a thin layer of cream cheese sat at my place.

"Wow!" I said. "Thanks, honey. This is so nice."

These breakfasts continued for a week. One morning, before they ended, I stood up in the middle of eating my bagel, walked to the other side of the room, grabbed a pen and paper, and returned to the table to begin a shopping list.

"No, Mama. Not now," Gabriel said. "We don't have much time before I leave for school."

"You're right," I said, and I pushed the pen and paper away.

Is that what happened? Or is that the way I want to remember it? What I do remember is feeling that I was the child and Gabriel the adult. Here was my son teaching me to be present. Mom, you can make a shopping list any time. Why must you do it now when we have only a few precious moments together before I go to school?

Not long thereafter, Gabriel reminded me yet again to be present. This time I was getting ready to leave our house to visit a woman in the hospital who had been living with terminal cancer for years. For some reason, I found myself searching for a gift to take her but couldn't find one. Usually when I visited this woman I just visited, but that day I wanted to bring her something. I voiced my predicament out loud. "I don't know what to bring to Dana when I visit her at the hospital today."

Gabriel's response "Mama, just bring yourself."

What does it mean to be present? Being present means not *just* doing or saying the right thing, not *just* writing the right words or appearing at the right time. Being present means being involved and engaged with a particular person at a particular moment in time, even if that person is us. Being present means not multitasking: not answering e-mails while we're talking on the phone, not texting one friend while we're having a conversation with another friend. It also means not multithinking: not letting our minds wander to our upcoming dinner party or to the package we need to drop off at the post office or to a disturbing exchange we had earlier in the day.

In his book *I and Thou*, philosopher Martin Buber speaks to the art of being present in our relationships. [59] According to Buber, to be present to another means to approach that person as a "Thou" in an "I-Thou" encounter. To be less than present to another means to approach the other as an "It" in an "I-It" encounter. An "I-It" encounter is often enacted as a means to an end. An "I-Thou" encounter is enacted as a means in and of itself. For example, when I hand my credit card to the cashier in the grocery store, this is an "I-It" encounter. I can elevate this "I-It" encounter to an "I-Thou" encounter if I engage in a deep conversation with the cashier during which I am present to her words.

---

59 Martin Buber, *I and Thou* (New York: First Scribner Classic/Collier Edition, 1987).

It's impossible for us to approach everyone we meet in an "I-Thou" encounter because it's impossible to be present toward everyone all the time. We can all probably recall times when we were not as present for another as we would have liked. We may even be able to recall the hurt we caused the other, perhaps even the hurt we caused ourselves. Remembering these times may make us feel sad or guilty, but this sadness or guilt is helpful only if it propels us to live more present to the people around us and more present to ourselves. Most of us can be present more of the time if we consciously choose to make being present a priority. The effort is worth it because, when we're present, not only do our relationships benefit, but we benefit, too: we find ourselves more whole.

In *Mortal Lessons*, Richard Selzer writes about a young man who made being present to his wife a priority. This man's wife had just had a tumor removed from her cheek. Selzer had been the surgeon. He had carefully followed the curve of this young woman's flesh to remove the tumor, yet he had severed a small facial nerve to the muscles of her mouth, and they remained "twisted in palsy, clownish." After surgery, Selzer stood on one side of this woman's hospital bed while her husband stood on the other. The woman asked Selzer if her mouth would remain this way. He answered that it would because of a cut nerve. She listened, took in the information, and remained silent. Her husband did not let the silence last for too long before he smiled and said, "I like it. It is kind of cute." About this man, Selzer writes, "All at once I *know* who he is. I understand, and I lower my gaze. One is not bold in an encounter with a god. Unmindful, he bends to kiss her crooked mouth, and I so close I can see how he twists his own lips to accommodate to hers, to show her that their kiss still works." [60]

My brother, Ari, made being present to me a priority. When I was twenty-five, I had a lump removed from my breast. As I unbandaged my

---

60   Richard Selzer, *Mortal Lessons: Notes on the Art of Surgery* (New York: Harcourt Brace 1996), 45–46.

wound and looked at it for the first time, all I saw was a large canyon filled with blood. I couldn't imagine it would ever heal. Ari, who was twenty at the time and studying to be a doctor, knew I was upset. He asked if he could look at the wound to see how it was doing. I nodded. "I know it looks terrible," he said, "but it will heal." Into the silence that followed, he added, "I know you think that no one will love you because of the scar, but don't worry, someone will." I'm not sure how he knew exactly what was bothering me, but he got it.

To be present when we're writing a forever letter means to be attuned to the person we're writing to. It means to imagine ourselves in an "I-Thou" encounter. When we write to another from this place of present-ness, we have a greater chance of being heard.

MEET A PERSON WHERE THAT PERSON IS

To meet a person where that person is requires us to be present but in a slightly different way. Let me explain what I mean by way of a story told by the Hasidic Master Rabbi Nachman of Bratslav.

There was once a king's son who believed he was a turkey. This boy would spend hours sitting naked under the dining room table picking at the leftovers that had fallen onto the floor. His worried father, the king, summoned doctors from all over the kingdom to help. Many came, but no one was able to help.

One day, a wise man showed up and offered his assistance. He wasn't a doctor. He possessed no medical knowledge and he knew nothing about remedies, but he was a wise man who understood the hearts and souls of people. This wise man did the only thing that made sense to him. He took off all his clothes, and he joined the king's son under the table. When the king's son asked him what he was doing, the wise man told the boy that he, too, was a turkey. The king's son was delighted to have the company of a fellow turkey, and so the wise man and the king's son hung out naked under the dining room table and got to know each other.

After a few days, the wise man asked that shirts be tossed down to them. He explained to the king's son that they could still be turkeys and wear shirts. Sometime later, the wise man had pants tossed down to them because they could wear pants and still be turkeys. He then had delicious food tossed down to them because they could eat delicious food and still be turkeys. Eventually, the wise man suggested that they sit at the table because they could sit at the table and still be turkeys. It was in this way that the wise man helped the king's son leave his turkey days behind and return to the world of humankind. [61]

By meeting the king's son "where he was," by joining him under the table as a turkey, this wise man earned the boy's trust and respect so that, when the time came and the wise man suggested a return to the table, the boy was ready to listen. When we meet a person "where he or she is," we have a greater chance of being heard.

Before I walk into a hospital room to visit someone after surgery, I try to imagine what that person may be feeling so that I can approach that person with care. When I meet with someone who has dementia, I try to imagine what it must be like to be unable to remember the facts I once knew and the people I once held dear so that I can approach that person with compassion and sensitivity. When I see a child kicking sand in the playground after having missed the final shot of the basketball game, I try to remember what it feels like to lose so that I can approach that child knowing the pain and loneliness of loss.

---

61   Francine Klagsbrun, *Voices of Wisdom: Jewish Ideals and Ethics for Everyday Living* (New York: Jonathan David Publishers, 1986), 184–185; and Y. David Shulman, *The Chambers of the Palace, Teachings of Rabbi Nachman of Bratslav* (Northvale, NJ: Jason Aronson, 1993), 1–2.

Amanda was in tears during a writing workshop. Tears are not uncommon during writing workshops, but as I watched Amanda, I sensed her tears were of a different sort. I walked over to see if she was okay. Amanda said she was stymied as to how to write a forever letter to her son, Bruce. She explained that, as a single mom, she and Bruce had been very close throughout his growing up, but that as a young adult he had felt the need to distance himself. He had recently married a woman of a different faith and had converted to that religion. Amanda was devastated. They talked about it, but there was tension. She wanted to write to him, but wondered whether he would even open the envelope once he saw that it was from her and, if he did open it, whether he'd read it with care or dismiss it.

Amanda and I spent time talking after the workshop. I asked her why she wanted to write to Bruce. Was it to re-establish their relationship, to create an opening for reconnection, to create a relationship with her daughter-in-law, to tell Bruce how much she loved him, to inspire Bruce to return to her faith, or to get angry with Bruce for leaving it? She had to be clear. If her reasons for writing were either of the last two, she would need to understand that she might not be meeting Bruce where Bruce was and that he might have trouble hearing her words.

We continued to talk about how she could write to her son and to her daughter-in-law to wish them well, to tell them how often she thought of them, how she knew that when the time came, they would be good parents and they would raise their children with strong values (as long as she meant it). We also spoke about how she could write a letter just to Bruce in a way that would neither condone his choices (because then she would not be being true to herself) nor condemn his choices (because then she would not be meeting Bruce where he was). I'm not sure what Amanda chose to do, but I did sense that she took in our conversation and that it enabled her to contemplate how best to approach her son in a way that would meet him where he was.

When we meet a person where that person is, we show that person that we understand him or her in a way that he or she might not have known that we did. Having made numerous attempts by phone to convince Gloria, her Seattle-based mother (who is not easy to convince as it is hard for her to travel and she likes her peace and quiet), to join the family on the East Coast for Passover and then stay on for a family bar mitzvah, Vicky decided to write her mother a letter so that she could raise and respond individually to what she understood to be her mother's concerns. Here's an excerpt from her letter:

> This is a chance, in the most simple way, to allow us the opportunity to show you how much we love and respect you, and give you the chance to sit in a room and look around at what you and Daddy produced. Families who are strong and healthy and have so much love to give.
>
> I know there may be reasons that come to your mind not to come. We've talked about them.
>
> If you are worried about gifts for the children ... I will have everything ready here for you to give each child from every family something. If you are worried about expense for travel ... I have a free companion ticket coming to me each year from Alaska airlines and I would love for you to be a "companion." If you are worried about health—We'll do our best to take care of you. You seem to be stronger than I ever remember you being. You have taken good care of yourself...
>
> I've also been thinking that you are the only great grandparent we all have. We need you to be here to represent Daddy (who would have loved this event) and to let us all hug you and give you love and respect. Please consider allowing us the chance to be together.

When I visited Gloria a few days after she received Vicky's letter, she showed it to me a bit offhandedly so as not to seem too enthusiastic, but I sensed her enthusiasm and celebrated it, acknowledging how special it was, how much she is loved, and how lucky she is. When I asked her how she felt when she received it, she responded: "I was speechless."

By meeting her mother where her mother was, Vicky succeeded in convincing Gloria to spend Passover with her family and to stay an extra week to join in the bar mitzvah celebration.

We can never be assured that our words will be heard in the way we want them to be heard, either verbally or in a forever letter, but we have a greater chance when we try to meet a person where he or she is, when we accept that person, and when we respect that person's choice, even if we disagree, and even if we, ourselves, would have made a different choice.

SHARE PERSONAL EXPERIENCES

Having had a tough first year of motherhood, Dorothy e-mailed a letter to friends after her son Elliott's first birthday, in which she shared her personal experience as a new mother coping with hard issues. Here's an excerpt:

> It has been an amazing and trying year for me. I struggled with anxiety and depression in a big way and though I have managed to stay afloat and to do a great job with raising Elliott during his first year, I have had to really privilege taking care of myself and our little family. This means that I didn't always do all the things I said I would do, like sending physical thank you cards, calling people or reaching out as much as I would ideally like to … 2013 was a year of hard labor, recovery, shifting and integrating new identities and roles as well as shedding old ones. It was a year of accepting limitations, reevaluating priorities, learning to let go

and embracing and welcoming the present in all of its beauty, wonder and richness.

Like Dorothy, we can share our personal experiences to explain ourselves to the people we love. We can also share our personal experiences with the people we love to help them better understand themselves. In the novel *Gilead* by Marilynne Robinson, seventy-six-year-old Reverend John Ames does both. Having been diagnosed with a failing heart and led to believe he has little time left on this earth, Ames writes a letter to his six- almost seven-year-old son in which he shares his personal experiences not only to explain himself but also to enable his son to better understand himself. An example of this is when Ames writes about his temper. After stating that he comes from preachers on both his mother's and father's side, he writes, "They were fine people, but if there was one thing I should have learned from them and did not learn, it was to control my temper. This is wisdom I should have attained a long time ago. Even now, when a flutter of my pulse makes me think of final things, I find myself losing my temper, because a drawer sticks or because I've misplaced my glasses. I tell you so you can watch for this in yourself." [62]

What a gentle way to share a personal experience. Here's a shortcoming of mine. I'm not happy about it, but I'm aware of it, and I try to not let it get the best of me. If you find, someday, that you, too, have this shortcoming, know from where it comes. Don't let it get the best of you. Be self-aware, and let your self-awareness help you to influence your actions for the good.

Sharing our personal experiences also enables us to reflect on the accomplishments of a loved one who is so much farther along on her path than we had been on our path at that same age. In "Letter to a Daughter at Thirteen," novelist and essayist Barbara Kingsolver does just that. She

---

62   Marilynne Robinson, *Gilead* (New York: Farrar, Straus Giroux, 2004), 6.

watches her daughter, who seems so comfortable with herself, her friends, and the clothes she wears that Kingsolver wonders how she ended up with such a "cool" daughter when she herself had been such an awkward teenager. She writes:

> You have confidence and wisdom beyond anything I'd found
> at your age. I thought of myself, at thirteen, as a collection of
> all the wrong things: too tall and shy to be interesting to boys.
> Too bookish. I had close friends, but I believed if I were a better
> person I would have more. At exactly your age I wrote in my
> diary, "Starting tomorrow I'm going to try to be a better person.
> I have to change. I hope somebody notices." ... My journal
> entries were full of a weirdly cheerful brand of self-loathing.
> "Dumb me" was how I christened any failure, regardless of
> its source. [63]

A final reason for sharing our personal experiences is to try to help free the people we love from the difficult places they find themselves in. Here's an excerpt from a forever letter that Simone, in her fifties, wrote to her twenty-four-year-old son, Patrick, who at the time of her writing, was feeling a lot of self-hatred and was stuck in a rigid frame of mind. Simone wanted to help him understand that his self-hatred wasn't helping him, and she wanted to give him insight into her negative thinking as a way to help free him from his own.

She writes:

> In my thirties, I finally made a few friends. I began to realize
> then that everyone who lives has faults and makes mistakes.
> Everyone. And what works for me now is to try not to dwell too
> much on my faults and mistakes (and the faults and mistakes of

---

63   Barbara Kingsolver, "Letter to a Daughter at Thirteen," in *Small Wonder* (New York: Perennial, 2003), 145.

others) but slowly, over time, try to learn to be just a little bit better. And—something I've learned from you—it really helps to figure out what your strengths are and use those to help you get where you want to be. Sometimes it helps me to think of what makes a good fictional character. Characters who are all good are boring … So I try not to be too hard on myself, but to keep in mind that I'm a person with a mixture of qualities in me, and other people are the same. We've talked about how everyone has a dark side. Some people repress it and some people channel it and some people let it run amok. I think it's best to acknowledge it and channel it.

Simone said that, not long after she gave Patrick this letter, his life got much better. She's sure it was a combination of things but wonders if her words helped.

When we share our personal experiences in a forever letter, we invite the people we love into our lives so that they can better understand us and can perhaps come to better understand themselves. We do this not to convince them to make the same choices in their lives that we made in ours, though we might hope they do. Nor do we do this to push our lives on them or to lay a heavy trip on them. We do this to explain ourselves, to connect, and to make an offering of love that we hope will help our words to be heard from a place of love.

BE OPEN, BE VULNERABLE

As a daughter, sibling, friend, wife, mother, teacher, rabbi, and chaplain, I've learned over the years to be vulnerable. When I'm vulnerable—by that I mean, when I unmask, when I'm open, when I'm self-revelatory—I encourage others to be vulnerable. By being myself in all of my humanness, I encourage others to be themselves in all of their humanness.

After Rafi died, I often ended up in uncomfortable interactions because people weren't sure how to respond when I told them that my brother had died. Here's what would happen: I'd meet someone new. We'd begin to talk. Invariably this person would ask, "How many brothers and sisters do you have?" I'd say, "I have two: My sister, Sarina, and my brother, Ari. I had another brother, Rafi, who died of cancer." At this point, most people would change the topic. I was surprised. I had thought that the majority might respond by saying things like, "I bet that was hard," or "I'm so sorry," or "What was that like for you?" At first I was hurt, but after this happened numerous times, I realized that these people, good people, were not trying to hurt me. They were either trying to avoid the sadness and fear that my loss brought up for them or they were trying to protect me from having to reenter the painful place of my loss.

Upon making this discovery, I realized I had a choice. When people asked me how many siblings I had, I could just mention my two living siblings, so as not to cause them discomfort. Or, I could invite them into the discomfort by saying things like, "I'm comfortable talking about him, so you can ask me questions," and "I like talking about him, even if it makes me sad, because it helps me remember him." You know what? People took me up on my invitation. They began to enter the place they feared, asking me questions, responding to me in my vulnerability, and sharing their vulnerability with me.

Remember the story I told a few chapters back—the story about not doing justice to my mother when I wrote the speech I would deliver at Park Avenue Synagogue? Well, a couple days after delivering that speech, I facilitated a writing workshop during which I shared that story about writing my speech, my father's gentle reprimand, my mother's hurt, and how devastated I felt.

After the workshop, a woman in her sixties approached me in tears. This story hit her in a deep way. She said she was dealing with a similar issue, a son whom she felt did not respect or appreciate her. She spoke about how she had recently attended a dinner during which he spoke and made flippant remarks about her. She was hurt and she didn't know what to do. I suggested that she talk to her son, much like my father had spoken to me. "You're still your son's mother," I said, "and you can still offer him guidance."

I bring this up because I remember pausing before I told my story that day, wondering if I was being too vulnerable by sharing my failings, but I went with my gut. I'm convinced that sharing my story enabled this woman to share her story, and maybe, just maybe, our conversation gave her the strength to reach out to her son.

When people speak to me as a rabbi or chaplain, they often say, "Rabbi, I'm sure you've seen this many times before." Early in my rabbinic career, I thought people said this because they wanted me to assure them that, though I was young, I was not new to the issues they were raising; but when people continued to say this to me after I'd been a rabbi for ten, fifteen, even twenty years, I realized they were saying this because they wanted to know they were not alone in their vulnerabilities, but that others were vulnerable, too.

We try to hide from our vulnerabilities, because we think that when we are vulnerable we are weak, but I believe that what we most want is not to hide; what we most want is to know that we're not alone, that others are vulnerable, too. Brené Brown, author of *Daring Greatly: How the Courage to Be Vulnerable Transforms the Way We Live, Love, Parent, and Lead*, has this to say about being vulnerable: "Vulnerability isn't good or bad: It's not what we call a dark emotion, nor is it always a light, positive experience. Vulnerability is the core of all emotions and feelings. To feel is to be vulnerable. To believe vulnerability is weakness is to believe that feeling is weakness. To foreclose on our emotional life out of a fear that the costs will be too high is to walk away from the very thing that gives purpose and meaning to living." [64]

When we write a forever letter from a place of vulnerability, we make an unmistakable statement about the seriousness of our intention to truly

---

64   Brené Brown, *Daring Greatly: How the Courage to Be Vulnerable Transforms the Way We Live, Love, Parent, and Lead* (New York: Gotham Books, 2012), 33.

connect with the people we love. By sharing our inner selves, by showing that our words come from a place of humility, where we all navigate life's trials together, rather than from a place where we think we know best, we increase our ability to be heard. When the people we love see that we've grown from visiting our own difficult places, we give them the courage to do the same.

STATE HARD TRUTHS WITH LOVE

Some of us may find ourselves wanting to state hard truths in our forever letters. Stating hard truths need not be harsh, demeaning, or absent of love. We can state hard truths in a gentle, positive, loving and compassionate tone, and by so doing we may enable the people we love to make important and necessary changes in their lives. It may be just the nudge a brother needs from his sister to get his life back on track, just the nudge a friend needs to extricate herself from a difficult relationship, or just the nudge a mother needs from her son the doctor to believe she can heal. It was just the nudge I needed from my father to write a more appropriate paragraph about my mother.

In Herman Wouk's World War II novel *The Caine Mutiny*, Dr. Keith, who has been diagnosed with malignant melanoma and given less than a month to live, writes a last letter to his young adult son Willie, who is headed back to the Navy to join the crew of the USS *Caine*. To me, this letter is a good example of stating hard truths in a way that can be heard, because *before* Dr. Keith states the hard truths he believes Willie needs to hear, he revisits his own life and comes to terms with his own hard truth—feeling that he missed out by going into private practice instead of following his heart and going into research. In the words below, he turns his attention to Willie:

> Perhaps because I know I'll never see you again I find myself
> sentimentalizing over you, Willie. It seems to me that you're
> very much like our whole country—young, naïve, spoiled and

softened by abundance and good luck, but with an interior hardness that comes from your sound stock. This country of ours consists of pioneers, after all, these new Poles and Italians and Jews as well as the older stock, people who had the gumption to get up and go and make themselves better lives in a new world. You're going to run into a lot of strange young men in the Navy, most of them pretty low by your standards, I daresay, but I'll bet—though I won't live to see it—that they are going to make the greatest Navy the world has ever seen. And I think you're going to make a good naval officer—after a while. After a great while, perhaps.

This is not criticism, Willie, God knows I am pretty soft myself. Perhaps I'm wrong. You may never make a naval officer at all. Perhaps we're going to lose the war. I just don't believe it. I think we're going to win, and I think you're going to come back with more honor than you believed possible.

I know you're disappointed at having been sent to a ship like the *Caine*. Now, having seen it, you're probably disgusted. Well, remember this, you've had things your own way too long, and all your immaturity is due to that. You need some stone walls to batter yourself against. I strongly suspect you'll find plenty of them there on the *Caine*. I don't envy you the experience itself, but I do envy you the strengthening you're going to derive from it. Had I had one such experience in my younger years, I might not be dying a failure.

Those are strong words, but I won't cross them out. They don't hurt too much and, furthermore, my hand isn't the one to cross them out any more. I'm finished now, but the last word on my life rests with you. If you turn out well, I can still claim some kind of success in the afterworld, if there is one...

Think of me and of what I might have been, Willie, at the times in your life when you come to crossroads. For my sake, for the sake of the father who took the wrong turns, take the right ones, and carry my blessing and my justification with you.

I stretch out my hand to you. [65]

These days, we seem to have a harder time confronting the people we love, especially our children, with hard truths. Maybe because we seek to be more lenient with our children than our parents were with us, or because we live in a time where the trend has inclined more to coddling our children than to confronting them. Maybe because we so want to protect them from the hurts, pains, and disappointments that are part of life, we forget that in so doing we are robbing them of the experiences that toughen their resolve and strengthen their character. But it's not only our children we have trouble confronting. It's difficult for us to express hard truths to anyone we love and care about. I think, on some unconscious level, it's because we're afraid that if we state hard truths, we'll somehow be communicating hurt rather than love to the people we love.

Living in a society where we're more psychologically attuned to the emotional weight of our words than those writing in the centuries before us, we understand that it's not just about the words we use, but it's also about the tone we choose. Tone is subtle, but it's what invites us in or what pushes us away. We know tone when we read it, hear it, and see it in the facial expressions and body language of others. The thing about tone is that, while we can detect it in others, it is often elusive, subtle, and hard to detect in ourselves, especially in our own writing. We must therefore take extra care to state our hard truths in a loving tone so that we have a greater chance of being heard.

---

65 Herman Wouk, *The Caine Mutiny* (Garden City, NY: Doubleday, 1951), 59–62.

ADD QUOTES

If your beliefs are dictated by your religious faith, consider including quotes from your tradition in your forever letter to highlight a belief. For example, if loving people and treating people with respect is a belief you want to pass on, and you come from the Judeo-Christian tradition, you might quote Leviticus 19:18: "Love your fellow as yourself." [66] If you're Jewish you might also quote the Sage Hillel, who rendered the Leviticus quote in the negative when he said, "What is hateful to you, don't do to your fellow." [67] If you're Buddhist, you might quote Udana-Varga 5:18: "Hurt not others in ways that you yourself would find hurtful." [68] If you're Hindu, you might quote one of these Hindu sayings: "Never do to others what would pain yourself" [69] or "One should not behave towards others in a way which is disagreeable to oneself." [70] If you're Muslim, you might quote from the hadith of Al-Nawawi: "None of you [truly] believes until he loves for his brother what he loves for himself." [71] You get the point.

If you're not a scholar and you want to include quotes from your tradition that speak to your beliefs, how do you find them? There are many places to search online. Go to one of the search engines (Google, Bing, Yahoo!, et cetera). Type in "quotes on peace in Christianity" (or in Judaism, Islam, Buddhism, etc.) or "quotes on compassion" or "quotes on faith" or quotes on whatever value you want to impart; you'll find mate-

---

66   *Tanakh: The Holy Scriptures, The New JPS Translation According to the Traditional Hebrew Text* (Philadelphia: The Jewish Publication Society, 1988), Lev. 19:18.

67   Shabbat 31a, trans. Elana Zaiman

68   Udana-Varga 5:18, in Lewis Browne, *The World's Great Scriptures* (London: Macmillan, 1946), 15.

69   Panche Tantra 3.104, in Roger Whiting, *Religions for Today* (London: Stanley Thornes, 1991), 97.

70   Mahabharata (Anusasana Parva 113:8), in James A. Long, *Expanding Horizons* (Pasadena, CA: Theosophical University Press, 1990), 61.

71   Hadith 13, Imam al-Nawawi, bible-quran.com/hadith-13-imam-nawawi-isla/.

rial. You can also find books within your tradition that highlight particular themes, subjects, or verses. In the Judeo-Christian tradition, for example, you can look up any word in a concordance and find the biblical verses in which this word is used. You can find other resources, too. Just ask you pastor, priest, imam, minister, rabbi, or elder for guidance.

Over the years, a number of people have told me they've discovered highlighted passages and handwritten notes in the blank pages of their parents', grandparents', or friends' bibles. One man told me that he cherishes a bible he received from his father with Post-it Notes marking the verses his father had found meaningful.

Whether or not you're a member of a religious tradition, you can always include quotes that have guided or inspired you throughout the years. If you're an avid reader, writer, musician, or artist, and you live by or have been inspired or influenced by a particular quote from a literary luminary, a musical master, or an august artist, consider sharing this quote in your forever letter, writing about what it has meant to you and how it has pushed you forward. Or, perhaps, it's the words of the people in your life whom you love and admire—your parents, grandparents, elders, teachers, mentors, children, siblings, friends—that you find yourself returning to. If so, consider sharing their words with the people you love.

Lisa, an artist friend who works in mixed media collage and assemblage, collects quotes and on occasion uses them in her work. One of her favorite quotes is from the novelist Kurt Vonnegut: "To practice any art, no matter how well or badly, is a way to make your soul grow. So do it." [72] As an artist she resonates with Vonnegut's advice because it's a pragmatic yet hopeful expression of the artistic endeavor and frees her from the thinking that every work she creates must be a masterpiece. Since this quote is central to her being, she could include this quote in a forever

---

72   Kurt Vonnegut, *A Man Without a Country* (New York: Seven Stories Press, 2005), 24.

letter, articulating how it speaks to her and how it could speak to the person or persons to whom she is writing.

When I spoke about the tradition of writing forever letters with a woman who was dying of cancer, she mentioned this saying from her father: "Remember you are just as good as anyone else. You are not better, but you are just as good." She recalled him saying these words to her from the time she was ten until well into her adulthood. I believe she even quoted them to her children. To have included these words that had influenced her so profoundly in a letter to her children, grandchildren, nieces, friends would have been to pass on the gift of the words themselves, and a piece of her father as well.

In one of my workshops, a woman in her late fifties recalled her grandmother's words to her when she was ten. "Margaret-Ann, you have the happy faculty of making people want to do things for you. Don't abuse it." Margaret-Ann recognized the truth of her grandmother's words when they were first uttered, and she continues to recognize their truth to this day. She understood that her grandmother was pointing out her gift and teaching her to use it wisely. If Margaret-Ann were to write a forever letter to someone, especially to someone who exhibited similar gifts, she could certainly quote her grandmother's words.

Tracy was in her late forties when she sat next to me on an airplane and told me about an important lesson she had learned from her father, who had been diagnosed with prostate cancer shortly after her mother had been diagnosed with endometrial cancer. She said that her father had agreed to be treated only so that he could take care of her mother. "It was hard," she said, "to have both parents suffering from cancer and nearing the end of their lives at the same time. My father sensed my anguish and comforted me with the words: 'I've never met a soul who's got around dying. You have to die of something.'"

Tracy's father's words reminded her to keep on living despite her sadness, helplessness, and fear. But that's not all. It was to her father's words that she returned when she was diagnosed with cancer. Today, Tracy's approach to life and to living with cancer is to live as intensely as possible and to be grateful for each day. Were Tracy to write a forever letter, she could quote her father's words and speak to how pivotal these words were in helping her cope with her parents' dying, her own cancer, and her understanding death as a part of life.

In some cases, when we show that there's a deeper history to what we want to transmit, and that our beliefs are not ours alone but are based in something larger than ourselves, we have a greater chance of being heard. One caveat: Too many quotes in our forever letter will have the opposite effect. The purpose of using quotes is to deepen our voice, not to be a stand-in *for* our voice.

INCORPORATE STORIES

Telling stories in a forever letter is a wonderful way to impart our beliefs because, when people receive guidance within the context of a story, they are offered a different way, often a more indirect way, and at times a less-threatening way, to take in a message. Traditional stories, family stories, personal stories, legends, tales, or fables are all fair game.

Let's say you're writing a forever letter to your nephew, who moves through life rather indifferently and you want to communicate to him the importance of appreciation, you could summarize the movie *Groundhog Day*, starring Bill Murray, the weatherman who is condemned to live the same day of his life over and over again until he gets it right. To explain what you mean when you say, "until he gets it right," you could write: until he learns to appreciate his life and the people around him, for only then is he able to move on to the next day, and only then is he able to experience a life of meaning.

The inspirational author Arthur Gordon tells a great story about his father who had promised to take him (thirteen) and his brother (ten) to the circus, when an urgent call came requesting their father's presence back at the office. As Arthur and his brother anticipated being let down, they heard their father say that he would not be coming into the office. Their mother offered their father an out: "The circus keeps coming back, you know." But their father wouldn't hear of missing the circus. "I know," he said. "But childhood doesn't." [73] Were Arthur to write a forever letter to someone he loved or admired, he could include this story about his father to highlight the importance of setting priorities and putting family first.

My uncle Charles told me a story that was so hard for him to tell; he had to pause a few times to keep from crying. He was in his twenties. It was the time of the Vietnam war. Before he left for the army, he asked his parents to leave the porch light on for him the whole time he was away. Wanting to be sure his parents followed through, he asked his fiancée, Rebecca, to drive by his house at different times during the day and night to see if the porch light was on. She wrote to him that it was. Envisioning that lit porch light comforted him during what was a grueling basic training. Were he to write a forever letter, he could certainly include this pivotal story, interpreting it as the need to create a visual reminder in our lives for the people we love or as the need to follow through on our word. No doubt he could pull any number of lessons from this story.

Joan, my husband's stepmother, grew up in Salt Lake City, Utah, in a typical middle class family with no money for expensive trips, though she never felt deprived. On spring breaks her parents would take her and her sister and brothers on camping trips in Utah and Nevada. They would pack up the car with their tents and cooking ware and sleeping bags and gallons of water and always head to a new destination determined by the maps her father requested from the Utah Geological Society. With each destination came a new treasure hunt. Who could find the most trilobites,

---

73 Arthur Gordon, *A Touch of Wonder* (Old Tappan, NJ: Fleming H. Revell, 1974), 86–87.

petrified wood, dinosaur bones, snowflake obsidian, topaz, rose quartz, or quartzite? Between treasure hunts, Joan's father taught them about the cactus, wildflowers, insects, and animals in the area. The values Joan learned from her family vacations: the importance of family time, the love of nature, a respect for the earth, and that money doesn't matter. Were Joan to write a forever letter to her son Matthew, she could write about these trips with her parents, the values these trips instilled in her, and how she chose to raise Matthew with similar values.

One final story: I was in my early thirties, naked, and sitting in the steam room in the women's locker room at the 92nd Street Y in Manhattan. When I entered, two women were already inside enjoying the steam. I introduced myself and inquired about them. Eventually, one of the women tired of the heat and left. I continued to talk with the other woman who was in her early sixties. We talked for only five minutes before she said to me: "I was once like you. I was enthusiastic and outgoing. I talked to everyone, but as I got older, I had to pull back. I realized that I was giving away all my energy. I didn't understand that I had to save some for myself."

At the time, I didn't understand where she was coming from, and I felt sad for her, sad that she had to pull back, and that she couldn't figure out how to be as fully engaged in the world as she had once been. It was only after turning forty-nine and having some health issues that I came to a similar conclusion. I understood that if I was going to be there for Seth and Gabriel and have enough energy left for myself by the end of the day, I needed to pull back a little from my intense and wholehearted engagement with the world.

If I told this story in a forever letter, I might introduce it by writing: "Sometimes teachers appear when we least expect them, and we must remember to be open to their teachings even if we don't quite understand them at the time." Or I might tell this story and conclude it by writing: "Now, as I get older I understand how important it is to hold onto my energy so that I'm not depleted. I hope you come to understand that you can hold on to some of your energy, that you don't have to give all your energy away."

You get the point. The purpose of telling stories in our forever letters is to highlight what we most want to impart. We can tell a story about the first time we learned what was most important to us, or we can write about an experience we think the person we're writing to will benefit from hearing, or we can tell a story about a quality we admire in the person we're writing to.

Stories are powerful. Telling a story about someone acting with compassion will resonate more deeply than writing, "be compassionate." Telling a story about living fully will resonate more deeply than writing, "live fully." Telling a story about humility will resonate more deeply than writing, "be humble." Telling a story about holding onto our vital energy will resonate more deeply than writing, "hold onto your vital energy." Why? Stories engage us, ground us, and go straight to the heart. We relate personally to stories and we remember stories. Stories are humanizing. Stories enable us to share our experiences in a gentle and indirect way.

BESTOW BLESSINGS

What is a blessing? I consider a blessing to be this: loving and supportive words we offer to someone we care about through which we focus wholly on that person's well-being. I believe that, when we bless another, we not only strengthen the person we're blessing but we strengthen ourselves. I also believe that the more comfortable we are speaking our blessings, the more comfortable we will become writing our blessings.

Hearing the word *blessing*, many of us think *God*. But it is possible to bless one another without mentioning God's name. "Hold on to What is Good" is a Pueblo poem I consider one such blessing:

Hold on to what is good
even if it is
a handful of earth.
Hold on to what you believe
even if it is
a tree which stands by itself.
Hold on to what you must do
even if it is
a long way from here.
Hold on to life even when
it is easier letting go.
Hold on to my hand even when
I have gone away from you.[74]

In 1988, when I was twenty-six, I received a blessing from my seventy-six-year-old New Rochelle–based grandmother. I had been contemplating whether to start rabbinical school in New York, where I was living, or move to Los Angeles and start rabbinical school there. I brought my dilemma to my grandmother. I laid out the pros and cons of moving. One of the biggest cons was moving further away from her. There were others: financial, familial, and communal. The truth is that, had I been making the decision logically, I would have stayed in New York, but my decision was not logical. Something in my heart was telling me to go to Los Angeles. My grandmother considered my conundrum for only a moment before she said, "You must listen to your heart." With these words she empowered me in a loving way to do what I wanted to do. She gave me her blessing, even though it meant letting me go.

---

74   Nancy C. Wood, "Hold on to What Is Good," *Many Winters: Poetry and Prose of the Pueblos* by Nancy C. Wood (Garden City, NY: Doubleday, 1974), 78.

When I planned to take a year's sabbatical to write this book, the elders at the retirement community where I serve as a chaplain also gave me their blessings even though it meant letting me go. How afraid I had been that they would be angry with me for deserting them, but after I had made my announcement and looked out at the sea of faces, I saw Bridget, in her eighties, an artist with whom I had many conversations about the need to create, raise her right hand high in the air to cheer me on. Others spoke up. They wished me well. They came over to me. They hugged me and kissed me and said they would miss me. When the room emptied, Bridget reappeared. She said, "You know our pact. You said you'd write, and I said I'd get back to my art. Now that you're writing, I have to get back to my sculpting."

Over the next few weeks, people offered me their blessings in person and in writing. Here are a few: "I'm proud of you. I'm glad you're doing this if it's what you want to do. So many people wait until it's too late." "You are a very brave lady to follow your dream. So few people have the strength to do this, and you are doing it with grace!" "That you will be missed goes without saying. That you have the chance to accomplish the dream of a lifetime—what can I say other than 'Go to it!'"

I believe that most of us yearn to receive blessings from the people we love. I find myself close to tears every time I read about Esau when he learns that his father, Isaac, has given away his blessing to his brother, Jacob. He wails. "Bless me too, Father!" he says. Isaac responds that his brother has taken his blessing. Esau then asks, "Have you not reserved a blessing for me?" After Isaac says there is nothing he can do, Esau asks again, "Have you but one blessing, Father? Bless me, too, Father!" Esau wails until his father blesses him. [75]

---

75 *Tanakh: The Holy Scriptures, The New JPS Translation According to the Traditional Hebrew Text* (Philadelphia: The Jewish Publication Society, 1988), Gen 27: 34, 36, 38.

Jacob, who receives his father's blessing, doesn't seem all that happy having received it, knowing that he has duped his brother to get it. At least that's how I read the text. On his way to meet Esau, after serving Laban for twenty years, Jacob wrestles with a man (angel). What is it that Jacob wants from this wrestling match? He wants a blessing. To this man (angel) Jacob says, "I will not let you go until you bless me." I believe Jacob seeks this blessing because he needs a blessing he has earned, a blessing meant solely for him, not a blessing he has stolen. It's interesting to me that both Esau and Jacob had to solicit their blessings. How much more meaningful it would have been for each of them to have received their blessings unsolicited.

When Jacob and Esau finally meet up and Jacob wants to convince his brother to accept the presents he has brought, the Hebrew word used is *barech*, bless. Jacob essentially says to Esau, "Take you my blessing." Though in English this exchange is often translated as *present* or *gift*, it's important in this context to take note of the Hebrew. The story between brothers thus concludes with Jacob giving his brother not just material gifts but an unsolicited blessing, one that Jacob could now give because he had earned his very own blessing from his wrestling match with the man (angel), a blessing that was rightfully his. Having been blessed, Jacob was now able to bless.

Ethan, in his fifties, said that he learned about the importance of passing on words of blessing to his children from his grandfather who never did. As a child, he kept hearing from others how proud his grandfather was of him, but he never heard these words directly from his grandfather. One day he confronted his grandfather, who responded: "You don't need to hear all that from me. You just need to keep doing what you do. You know I love you and I'm proud of you." But Ethan didn't know. Ethan needed to be told. Most of us need to be told. It's hard to read blessings into silence.

When we think about how meaningful it is for us to receive blessings from the people we love, we understand how important it is for us to offer blessings to the people we love. To include blessings in our forever letters indicates that we have attuned ourselves to the persons we are blessing and that we truly desire for them what they wish for themselves.

6

WHAT TO AVOID

*Strive to close the eyes of the body and open those of the soul
and look into your own heart.*

—TERESA OF AVILA[76]

In this chapter, I suggest five things to avoid when you write forever letters. I offer this guidance neither to stop you from writing nor to make you nervous about writing, but to encourage you to take great care to think about what you write and why you write it.

FAVORITISM

In Erma Bombeck's collection, *Motherhood: The Second Oldest Profession*, there's a story entitled, "What Kind of a Mother Would ... Die and Not

---

76   Teresa of Avila, *The Collected Works of St. Teresa of Avila*, vol. 2, trans. Keiran Kavanaugh and Otilio Rodriguez (Washington, DC: ICS Publications, 1980), 173.

Take You With Her?" It's about Julie, who dies of cancer at forty-eight and leaves behind three sons: Chuck, Steve, and Tim. The setting: Julie's church funeral. The scene: each son sitting quietly in his pew, recalling his relationship with his mother. Built into each son's reflection is the last letter his mother wrote to him in which she states how much she loves him and how he is her favorite. [77]

Bombeck got it. She understood that every child secretly yearns to be the most beloved or favorite child. Though this story is fiction, I found myself wondering what would have happened had these brothers shared their letters with each other. I imagine they would have laughed, understanding how it was possible for each of them to have been the most loved by their mother.

In my family we had an experience where favoritism could have become an issue. A number of years ago, my mother made a placemat, a collage of photographs of her children and grandchildren that she reproduced, laminated, and mailed to each of her grandchildren. When my son, Gabriel, received his placemat, I called my mother. "Mom," I said, "Gabriel just got his placemat. Thanks so much. But why are there fewer photos of him than of your other grandchildren?" "There aren't," my mother said. She was adamant. "I put in the exact same number of photographs of each of my grandchildren. I knew you would all count."

I was teasing my mother. I knew she wouldn't put in more photographs of one grandchild than another. I knew this because I know my mother. I also knew this because in her family of origin her parents played favorites, and there's no way she'd repeat that mistake. Her love for us all is present, palpable, and constant, though I do imagine there are times when my mother feels closer to one of us than another.

---

77   Erma Bombeck, *Motherhood: The Second Oldest Profession* (New York: McGraw-Hill, 1983), 68.

I mention the Erma Bombeck story and I tell this story about my family because, when we sit down to write our forever letters, we have options. We can write to an individual or to a group. Our decision will probably depend on our relationships with the persons to whom we're writing and on these persons' relationships with each other. It will also depend on how specific we want to be. For example, if we're writing to ask for forgiveness from someone, offering forgiveness to someone, or to address private matters, we will probably want to write to that individual alone. On the other hand, if our message is more general, we may consider writing only one letter and addressing it to all of the people we are writing to, for example to all of our family, or all of our students. We can always jot a personal note on each individual's letter.

Another approach to consider when writing a group letter is to include a personal paragraph for each member of the group. If we choose this approach, we must take care to devote the same amount of space to each person, keeping each person's paragraph the same length, and balancing the amount of praise and concern that we offer. How would it look if we wrote a loving paragraph to one person and a concerned paragraph to another? We must keep in mind that, when we write to a group, everyone will be reading everyone else's paragraphs, and that we're fooling ourselves if we don't think they'll compare their paragraphs and try to conclude which of them we love more. We must also keep this in mind: If we write lovingly about one person and less lovingly about another, it could set these individuals at odds with each other. I imagine this is not the legacy we want to leave.

COMMANDING WITH THE PEN

There's an expression in the legal profession: do not rule from the grave. Lawyers often pass these words on to their clients who are writing last will and testaments. This expression means what we think it means: We should not make unreasonable, untenable, or unfair demands on the people we leave behind. It means that when we die, we should let go of our control and let our descendants live their own lives.

In *The Life of Meaning*, Bob Abernethy interviewed funeral director, poet, and essayist Thomas Lynch about mortality. Lynch spoke about the need to impart our values without controlling from the grave. As an example, he mentioned a letter that a young man had received from his father about what he thought appropriate for his funeral. He listed a hymn he liked, asked to be buried next to his wife, and so on. Lynch writes, "And at the bottom of the letter was a paragraph that I've always thought of as a kind of coupon. It was a disclaimer, and it said, 'I've felt, furthermore, that all this is done for the living. So, do whatever you want. It won't bother me one bit.' So, he had done both things. He had communicated his values without giving someone hoops to jump through."[78]

The idea of not ruling from the grave translates into a similar principle for the forever letter writer I have decided to call "do not command with the pen." It means not making unreasonable, untenable, or unfair demands on the people we love by telling them how to live their lives, by exacting promises that may be difficult for them to keep, or by creating situations that leave them with feelings of guilt and resentment.

Alicia told me that when she and her father had an end-of-life discussion, she had helped her father not to make such demands when she said to him: "Dad, what if I can't follow what you say? What if you say 'Take care of your siblings' and my husband is sick at the same time? What do I do then? What if you tell me to be there when you die, and I'm out of the country? It's not a fair position to put me in. Trust that when the time comes, I'll do what's right."

---

78   Thomas Lynch, "Limning the Rites of Death," Bob Abernethy and William Bole, eds., *The Life of Meaning: Reflections on Faith, Doubt, and Repairing the World* (New York: Seven Stories Press, 2008), 13.

These kinds of conversations happen not only at the end of life but throughout the course of our lives. When we tell our daughter whom she should or shouldn't marry, or whether she should or shouldn't have children, we command with words. When we tell our grandson that he should let go of his dream to become a poet because he will not be able to earn a livelihood, or when we tell our friend that she should give up her career and spend more time with her grandchildren, we command with words. When we give our seventy-five-year-old parents an ultimatum that they need to move across the country to be near us because we refuse to get on a plane every time something happens to them, even though they are still relatively young and in fine health, we command with words.

Similarly, we command with words when we impose our unlived wishes (or expectations) for ourselves upon others or when we attempt to recreate someone in our own image, both of which I believe we are guilty of more often than we're willing to admit. If a mother had wanted to be a musician but had not been allowed to follow that path, and she were to push that path on a daughter who had little interest in music, she would be commanding with words. If a brother told his sister who wanted to become a teacher that she had to join the family business, or if a professor told her physics student who wanted to become an architect that he had to become a physicist because of his brilliance in the field, they would be commanding with words.

When we put these words in writing, we command with the pen.

Don't get me wrong. I believe it's possible for parents, grandparents, siblings, spouses, aunts and uncles, children, teachers, students, mentors, and friends to offer guidance to the people they love, but this guidance should be expressed as a hope and not as a demand. No person should decide for any other person how that person should live. As we write forever letters to the people we love, we must understand that they have their own interests, dreams, values, and lives to live.

If only Elizabeth Gee had understood this. Elizabeth Gee was a woman who died of cancer in 1991. Before her death, she had the foresight to write letters to her daughter, Rebecca, for many of Rebecca's future birthdays. She left these letters in sealed envelopes for her husband to mail each year before Rebecca's birthday. [79]

Rebecca received her mother's first letter when she was seventeen and in college. At the time, she was feeling isolated and alone. Among the many things her mother wrote in this letter was: "You will never be alone. You will always have me." For these words, Rebecca was grateful. She was also grateful for her mother's stories relating what she had been doing at the same age, for her mother's words of love and support, and for her mother's encouragement to live her life to the fullest and to believe that she could succeed at whatever she chose to do.

As the years went on, though, Rebecca spoke to the downside of receiving her mother's letters. She said that in some letters her mother stated expectations that Rebecca couldn't fulfill: stay close to the church, be a Mormon woman, and marry a Mormon man. Her mother even wrote, "If you don't go to the temple, you won't go to heaven. You're not going to see me." Because Rebecca had moved away from the Mormon Church, she felt that she had disappointed her mother. She also felt angry with her mother for holding her to beliefs that she no longer held, and she began to dread opening her mother's letters, fearing that they would be filled with requests she couldn't honor.

Some of you might consider this reason enough not to write a forever letter. You might think, "Why bother writing if I can get myself into trouble?" Don't use this story as an excuse not to write. Think about how Elizabeth's first letter helped Rebecca move forward with her life.

---

79   David Segal, interview with Rebecca Gee, "Parent Trap," episode 401 of *This American Life*, Chicago Public Media, February 19, 2010, www.thisamericanlife.org /radio-archives/episode/401/parent-trap.

Dave understood what it meant not to command with the pen when he wrote in his forever letter, "In my Last Will and Testament, I have given my family all of my material possessions. In this document, I seek to give you something more important and lasting. If you, as the reader, have a concern that I am somehow attempting to impose myself on you (or the way you are living your life), you need not worry. I only intend to pass on some lessons I have learned over a lifetime—not to seek to control yours."

The poet Christian Wiman also succeeded in not commanding with the pen. In his moving essay "Mortify Our Wolves," Wiman writes about his daily fight against a rare form of cancer, his rediscovery of his Christianity, and his continued belief in God despite his diagnosis. Toward the end of his essay, he addresses his twin daughters: "But if you find that you cannot believe in God, then do not worry yourself with it." [80]

Most of us do not purposefully seek to command with the pen, nor do we purposefully seek to hurt the people who matter to us most. So when we write a forever letter, we must take great care to write in a way that enables us to be true to ourselves and to honor and respect the people we love, who need to live their own lives, follow their own paths, face their own failures, delight in their own successes, and live into the selves they're on the road to becoming. There's a fine line between imparting our values and telling others what to do, but with finesse and care, it's possible to strike the right balance.

TELLING FAMILY SECRETS

Imagine a mother grappling with the following dilemma: She's writing a forever letter to her daughter. The two of them are close, but there's a secret that her daughter doesn't know: Her daughter is not her husband's daughter but the daughter of a man with whom she had an affair.

---

80   Christian Wiman, "Mortify Our Wolves," *The American Scholar,* Autumn 2012, 71.

What should this mother do? Should she write about this secret? Forever letters are about passing on values. Perhaps as she contemplates her life and her values, she feels guilty for keeping this information a secret for as long as she has. Or perhaps she has recently learned that her daughter's father has early onset Alzheimer's, and she wants her daughter to be aware of this medical information.

There are many reasons this mother might want to share her secret with her daughter, but before doing so, she might want to ask herself these questions: Why am I choosing this venue for sharing my secret? When do I plan to give this letter to my daughter? Before I die? Or will I leave it for her to find after my death? Do I plan to share my secret with my husband? If not, does it matter to me if my daughter shares my secret with him, presuming he is still alive? How will he feel hearing about my affair from my daughter, whom he had also thought was his daughter? What effect will sharing my secret have on their relationship?

She also may want to try putting herself in her daughter's position and ask herself these questions: How would I feel reading about my mother's affair in a letter rather than hearing about it from her in person? How would it affect my memory of my mother if I were reading her words after her death? To whom would I address all of my unanswered questions? Questions like: Who is my real father? Is he still alive? Can I meet him? Does he know I exist, or did you not tell him, either? Why did you have an affair? Does Dad (meaning my current Dad, the only Dad I have ever known) know? If not, why didn't you tell him? Why didn't you tell me sooner? Why did you tell me at all? How could you keep this from me for all these years? What else you are hiding? How do I know when to trust you?

My suggestion: Don't share secrets in a forever letter. Don't use your forever letter as a platform to open a door that has been shut and locked for years. If you want to share a secret, it's best shared in person. Perhaps the person hearing the secret will have questions she'll want to ask you, or perhaps she'll erupt in anger and leave your presence immediately because she'll need time to process the information before asking you questions. Who knows? We never know what reaction our secret will spark. But if we unveil our secret in person and make it clear that we're willing to talk about it, we open up the possibility of connection and forgiveness.

How we deal with the secrets of our past can have a profound effect on how we live, parent, and communicate, and on the legacy we leave behind. How we choose to share these secrets can also have a profound impact on our lives and on the lives of the people we're closest to.

In her memoir, *Torch in the Dark*, Hadiyah Carlyle revealed that she had been raped by her father's employee in the basement of her father's store when she was three and a half. Her father found her, screamed at her, and told her to get back upstairs if she knew what was good for her. When she was fifteen, she wrote a paper for her science class about her family in which she mentioned this rape. Her parents were called into school, and the school psychologist proceeded to berate Carlyle in front of her parents for telling lies. Carlyle was given a C- for her paper, told to apologize to her parents after school, and to never speak of it again. [81]

Carlyle's memoir is not just about the revelation of this secret. It's about how this secret led her to live the life she lived: as a hippie, psychiatric patient, young single mother unsure of how to mother and how to make a living to support herself and her son, Reuben. Writing this memoir was her way of confronting herself and coming to terms with her past. It was her way of telling Reuben more about herself, her life, and their life together as mother and son. But Carlyle's memoir is not a forever letter.

Were Carlyle to write a forever letter to Reuben, I imagine she would write a very different document in which she would focus on articulating her values. Perhaps she would write about the value of telling the truth

---

81   Hadiyah Joan Carlyle, *Torch in the Dark* (Bothell, Washington: Book Publishers Network, 2012), 41–42.

and living the truth, no matter how hard it is and no matter how hard everyone tries to get you to deny it.

In *Stories for Boys*, Gregory Martin also writes about a secret. All Martin knew when he appeared at the hospital was that his father had overdosed. His mother had refused to tell him why, saying that he would have to wait for his father to wake up to hear the story from him directly, a story she had heard shortly before his overdose. In the hospital room after his father awakened from a thirty-six-hour coma, he told Martin that for the whole of his married life (thirty-nine years), he had been having affairs with men.

At the time Martin heard about his father's infidelities, he was a father with two young sons. When his parents divorced suddenly, Martin never told his sons why. Over time, this bothered him. He writes, "They were confused and sad, and I had an explanation, and I was keeping it from them, and this unspoken explanation was intimately related to other unspoken explanations—a chain of secrets and unacknowledged sadness that now ran through me to them." [82] Martin struggled with how and when to tell his sons, but he did, because he refused to keep his father's sexual orientation a secret from his sons as it had been kept a secret from him.

Martin wrote his memoir to help him digest, assimilate, and understand his father's story, and to help him heal from and make sense of the deception. He also wrote his memoir for his sons so that they would someday better understand their father. Were Martin to write a forever letter to his sons, he, like Carlyle, might write about the importance of truth-telling, or about having the courage to be honest even when we're ashamed, or about how no one is perfect and how we have to be careful how we judge one another.

82　Gregory Martin, *Stories for Boys* (Portland, OR: Hawthorne Books & Literary Arts, 2012), 80.

I appeared in Seth's life eight years after his father, Michael, had committed suicide. We married a year later. The story as I understand it: Michael had been depressed, he had assured those who cared about him that he would never commit suicide. Three weeks later he was dead. He had stopped his car on the Taft Bridge in Washington, DC, got out with the car still running and clothes from the dry cleaner hanging on the hook in the backseat, and he jumped. All who were close to him believed that the antidepressant he had been prescribed three weeks prior had taken him down.

One day, when Gabriel was about eight, he asked Seth how his father had died. Seth could have kept his father's suicide a secret, but he didn't. He told Gabriel the truth. He told Gabriel that his father had been unhappy and that he had been put on some medication to help him but that the medication hadn't helped; rather it seemed to have led his father to take his own life. They talked for a while. Seth answered all of Gabriel's questions. He let Gabriel know that anytime he had questions, he could ask. By presenting Gabriel with the truth, he communicated to Gabriel that his father's suicide was not something to be ashamed of. He also modeled for Gabriel the importance of honesty. Had Gabriel heard that Seth's father had committed suicide from someone else, I imagine he would have been hurt and angry that his own father hadn't told him. Had he read about Seth's father's suicide in a letter Seth had written, I imagine he would have been hurt and angry that Seth had not shared this with him in person.

Meg, in her mid-fifties, told me that before her mother died, her mother had alluded to the fact that Meg might have additional siblings. After her mother died, Meg's aunt confirmed it. From her experience living with family secrets, Meg made a conscious decision there would be no secrets in her family; she and her husband would be honest with their children about their lives and their past.

When we write forever letters to the people we love, we must remember that the forever letter is not the appropriate venue for sharing secrets; personal conversations are much more appropriate for this kind of sharing.

ENCOURAGING OTHERS TO LIVE THE VALUES WE NEVER LIVED

The Hasidic Master Rabbi Menachem Mendel of Kotzk taught, "If you truly wish your children to study Torah [the traditional teachings],[83] study it yourself in their presence. They will follow your example. Otherwise, they will not themselves study Torah but will simply instruct their children to do so."[84] The point is clear. If, as parents, we truly wish for our children to eat well, we must eat healthy meals. If, as personal trainers, we truly wish for our clients to understand the importance of exercise, we must exercise. If, as children, we truly wish for our parents to understand how important climate change is to us, we must reduce our carbon footprint. This holds for anything we care about and want to share.

This raises a question: Can we write forever letters to the people we love, encouraging them to live values we never lived, or is doing so hypocritical? I believe that we can encourage people to live values we have never lived, but, if we do, we must be honest about not having lived the values we're encouraging them to embrace.

Let's say that as we look back on our lives, we wish we had worked less and had spent more time with our children. We could certainly write to our children and express our hope that when they become parents, they don't follow our example, that we blew it, that we missed out. Or let's say that as we reflect on our lives in our mid-forties and see how making more

---

83   Explanation in brackets mine.

84   Menachem Mendel of Kotzk, *Amud Ha'Emet, Teachings, Sayings, Discussions and Life of Our Teacher R. Menachem Mendel of Kotzk*; ed. Moshe Betzalel Alter (Tel Aviv, Israel: Pe'er Publishing, 5760 [1999–2000]), 91.

money than our friends has been what has been most important to us, we may realize that our parents had it right all along, that sometimes less can be more. In this case, we could certainly write to our parents to tell them that we finally understand what it was they were trying to teach us and that we hope to begin to shift our lives in that direction.

Or maybe we tried to live according to certain values and failed. If that were the case, we could write: "So, these are the values I've tried to live. I haven't been as successful as I would have liked. Still and all, they are worthy values to try to live, and here's what I've learned from trying to live them … Perhaps you will do better than I did, and perhaps you will do a better job of living the values that are important to you."

By reflecting on our values, by being honest with ourselves about the values we've lived and the values we haven't, we stand in a better position to share our values and to encourage the people we love to live into their values.

LYING TO OTHERS, LYING TO OURSELVES

Sometimes we tell white lies so as not to hurt another person's feelings. We say things like, "That dress looks great on you," when in fact we think it is horrid, or "Yes, he's so handsome," when we do not find him the least bit attractive, but what difference does it make what we may think? If our friend finds him attractive, that's what counts; she is, after all, the one dating him. Besides, he seems like a lovely man. Or what about when the phone rings and we're not in the mood to talk, so we call out to our roommate, parent, spouse, or child, "If you pick up the phone and it's for me, I'm not home." There are probably many white lies we tell without considering ourselves to be liars because, after all, these lies do not really hurt anyone.

We still have to be careful, as Sissela Bok writes in her book *Lying: Moral Choice in Public and Private Life*: "Those who begin with white lies can come to resort to more frequent and more serious ones. Where some tell a few white lies, others may tell more. Because lines are so hard to draw, the indiscriminate use of such lies can lead to other deceptive practices. The aggregate harm from a large number of marginally harmful instances may, therefore, be highly undesirable in the end—for liars, those deceived, and honesty and trust more generally." [85]

Often we think of our white lies and even the more serious lies we may tell in the context of our relationships with others, but I want to think about these lies in the context of our relationship with ourselves.

As a young adult I had a friend, Lily, who was bulimic. On the one or two evenings a month we ate dinner together, I noticed that Lily would spend a lot of time after dinner in the bathroom. I became suspicious. Was it the toilet flushing one too many times? The lingering rancid odor in the bathroom? The remains of what looked like vomit in the toilet bowl? Probably all of these things. But what most convinced me of Lily's bulimia were the stories she created to cover up why she spent so much time in the bathroom. Had she said nothing, I might have been less suspicious. I knew Lily was lying to me, and I was sad. I wondered how she could lie to me, her good friend. What I came to understand was this: Lily wasn't lying to me. She was lying to herself. She needed to tell her stories, hear her stories, and believe her stories so that she could convince herself of their truth.

Gambling addicts, drug addicts, and alcoholics often lie to their families, friends, and colleagues about why they gamble, do drugs, or drink before they come to the realization that the lies they're telling others are really lies they're telling themselves to convince themselves that they're okay, that they don't have problems, that they don't need help.

---

85   Sissela Bok, *Lying: Moral Choice in Public and Private Life* (New York: Vintage Books, 1979), 63.

In her book *Drinking: A Love Story*, Caroline Knapp writes about how she denied her alcoholism, kept it compartmentalized, and convinced herself that she really didn't have a problem, because if she did, she'd be hiding a bottle in her desk, or drinking too much at night to make it into the office the next day or too much during her lunch hour to make it back to the office, or she'd be out of a job. [86]

Toward the end of her book, she writes, "Accordingly, a great deal of the active alcoholic's energy is spent constructing façades, an effort to present to others a front that looks okay, that seems lovable and worthy and intact. Inside versus outside; version A, version B. The double life grows more sophisticated and more deeply entrenched. Mostly, we lie. That's a statement of fact, not a judgment. Alcoholics lie about big things, and we lie about small things, and we lie to other people, and (above all) we lie to ourselves." [87]

For those of us who think we're exempt from lying to ourselves because we're not bulimic or gambling addicts, drug addicts, or alcoholics, we're fooling ourselves. There are many ways we lie to ourselves. What it comes down to are the stories we tell ourselves, the parts of our stories we choose to highlight and the parts we choose to withhold, the way we touch up or reframe our stories to make ourselves look better or others look worse, the way we shift our stories to hide our shame, guilt, arrogance, or greed, or the way we come to believe the stories we tell ourselves as truth.

Here are a few examples: When a niece idolizes her uncle as a breadwinner even though he's unable to hold down a job, she's lying to herself. When a mother tells herself she treats her son and daughter equally when in fact she favors her son, she's lying to herself. When a student delights in his teacher's brilliance but refuses to acknowledge his teacher's psychological problems, he's lying to himself. When a brother acknowledges his

---

86   Caroline Knapp, *Drinking: A Love Story* (New York: Delta Trade Paperbacks, 1996), 19.
87   Ibid., 193.

sister's generosity but is unable to see her disgust for those less fortunate than herself, he's lying to himself.

These ways of lying to ourselves often cause harm in our relationships, and not only in our relationships with the people we're lying to ourselves about but in other relationships as well. If I, as a mother, favor my son over my daughter, I'm causing harm not only to my daughter but also to my son, to my relationships with each of them, and possibly to their relationship with each other.

So how do we write a forever letter in which we take responsibility for the lies we lived that affected the people we love? Here's how: We tell our truth. We express our hurt, sadness, and disappointment in ourselves. Perhaps we even state our hope for reconciliation.

I've created three examples below to highlight what this truth-telling might look like.

This first example is an excerpt from a letter that I imagine a recovering alcoholic mother might write to her daughter:

> I'm an alcoholic. I started drinking shortly after you were
> born and continued until well into your teenage years. I don't
> remember most of your early life. I was living in such denial.
> I didn't realize how sick I was. I wish I could relive those years
> with you and be the mother I should have been. If there were
> a way, I'd do it in a second. I am so sorry. Please forgive me. I
> know this is a huge ask, especially since it has taken me years to
> forgive myself, and I'm not sure I completely have. As I write
> this, I'm imagining how I would respond if I were in your place,
> if my mother were asking for forgiveness from me. I'm not sure
> what I'd do.
>
> Despite me, you managed to grow up to be self-confident
> and loving, and you managed to find other role models. I was
> glad you adopted Charlie's family and spent so much time there.

I would love to get together with you. I want to hear all about you: all about the early years of your life that I missed because of my drinking, and all about what you're up to now. I understand it might take you time to decide how you want to respond. I understand that you may never respond. But I could not live with myself if I didn't try to reach out to you, if I didn't apologize, and if I didn't ask for your forgiveness.

This second example is an excerpt from a letter that I imagine a major-league baseball player might write to his grandson with whom he had little connection, as this grandson had no interest in baseball:

I told myself when I first became a grandpa that I would treat both of my grandsons equally. But now I see that I didn't do that. I was out there in the yard, playing ball with Andrew and taking him to ball games. I kept asking you to join us, but you weren't interested. I convinced myself that I was being a good grandpa because I kept asking and continued to respect your decision not to come, but the truth is I was glad you never came. I wouldn't have known what to say to you. I should have tried to connect with you in a way that was meaningful to you, like chess. You invited me to a number of your tournaments. You asked me to read chess books with you. You even offered to teach me how to play, but I never took you up on any of it.

Your grandmother used to needle me, tell me how I was so much more interested in Andrew because he loved baseball. I would get angry with her and tell her to stay out of my business. I told her she had no idea what she was talking about, but now I see that she was right. You're an adult, and I don't even know who you are because I never took the time to find out. I feel so bad about this. It eats away at me every day. Please forgive me. Is it too late? Can I try again?

This third example is an excerpt from a letter that I imagine a younger sister, now in her late forties, might write to her fifty-year-old brother, with whom she has had a difficult relationship from middle school and through much of their adult life:

I've been talking to my therapist about my childhood, and since you were a part of it, I've been talking about you, too. I've learned a lot about myself, most of which I'm not proud of, but here's what's relevant to us. In junior high school and in high school, I wanted to be cool and popular, but I wasn't as cool and popular as I wanted to be, and I blamed it on you. In my eyes, you were the reason. All you wanted to do was read your science books, do your crazy experiments, and hang out with other science nerds like yourself. My cool and popular friends thought you were a geek. You know because they made fun of you. And you know because I made fun of you, too. I felt I had no other choice, or at least that's how I saw it then. I so wanted to be liked by them that I did anything that I thought would make them like me, and joining them in making fun of you was one of those things. Truth is, there was a piece of me that was jealous of you. You had something you were curious and passionate about. I had nothing like that.

To this day, Mom and Dad fill me in on your research. They're so proud of you. I can't imagine what they tell you about me when you all talk. I think they're proud of my marketing position and that I make a good living. I know they love my husband and my kids, but I sense that they carry a deep disappointment regarding how I treated you when we were kids. I know they're hurt that we're not in contact with each other. Many times over the years, they suggested that I reach out to you, but I never did. I wasn't ready. I hadn't taken the time to look at myself and to take responsibility for my behavior.

What I want to say is this: I'm sorry for how I treated you when we were young. I'm sorry for not being able to face my own demons earlier. I love you, and I'm proud of all you have accomplished. I'm also in awe of how on some level, you didn't let all my teasing stop you from believing in yourself and from going on to achieve all you have achieved.

Writing a forever letter gives us the opportunity to let go of our lies and to be honest both with ourselves and with the people we love.

7

THOUGHTS ON THE WRITING PROCESS

*If we had to say what writing is, we would define it
essentially as an act of courage.*

—CYNTHIA OZICK [88]

This chapter offers suggestions about how to approach the writing process. Among the topics discussed: writing environment, writing tools, emotions that surface as we write, the need to prioritize the writing process, and writing partnerships.

---

88   Cynthia Ozick, qtd. in *Crafting Prose*, eds. Don Richard Cox and Elizabeth Giddens (San Diego, CA: Harcourt Brace Jovanovich, 1991), 9.

GET COMFORTABLE: PLACE AND PARAPHERNALIA

Decide in advance where you will write. Choose a place where you will have no distractions, where you can be quiet inside. This may be your home. This may be the coffee shop down the street. If you're able, silence your phone so you can be fully present.

Select a notebook you feel comfortable writing in. It need not be an expensive notebook. Better if it is not. This way you will not feel compelled to fill it with lavish handwriting or with only the most meaningful thoughts.

I like 8 x 10.5-inch spiral notebooks, college-ruled, with seventy sheets, because I don't mind throwing them away (which I do) when I have transferred their contents to my computer. I also like that they're not bound and that I can rip out the sheets I want to discard without causing other pages to fall out.

I also like college-ruled, bound composition books with a hundred sheets, those books with the black-and-white marbled cover. I appreciate the composition book because it's a little more compact and because, when I write in it, I feel as if I am journaling. The one disadvantage: it's impossible to rip out pages without compromising the notebook.

Select a pen you feel comfortable writing with. I prefer black because it's bold, gives weight and legitimacy to my words, and holds up over time. Whatever you do, don't write in light colored inks such as purple, pink, or red. These inks fade within five years.

Write on only one side of the notebook's pages. This way when you read over your material and you want to add in a thought, you can write that thought on the back of the previous page and draw an arrow to the place in your text where you want to insert it. You can also reference two or three pages at a time.

I know many people who compose on a computer because it's the only way they can think, or it's the way they learned to write, their handwriting is illegible, or they don't like the two-step process of writing longhand and then typing their words. I understand these reasons. At times I, too, prefer to compose on the computer. But for generating material and for writing the first draft of a forever letter, I prefer longhand. For me, there's something about putting pen to paper that makes the writing experience more personal. In the words of Norbert Platt, "The act of putting pen to paper encourages pause for thought, this in turn makes us think more deeply about life which helps us regain our equilibrium." [89] Never mind that Platt was once president and chief executive officer of Montblanc International, the fountain pen empire. He understood the power of the pen meeting the page.

I think of writing longhand in this way: it's as if there are a series of veins that begin in our writing fingers—our thumb, index, and middle finger—that end in our heart, enabling us to tap more deeply into our emotions. The rabbis of old believed there was a direct connection between the index finger and the heart. That's why to this day during a Jewish wedding ceremony the groom places a wedding ring on his bride's index finger. The bride can transfer this ring to her ring finger following the ceremony.

Another reason to write longhand is that the most important part of this initial phase of writing is to get our heart—the conscious and the unconscious—on the page. When we write longhand, we don't feel as compelled to edit as we write, correct every word that's not precise, every feeling that's not expressed to perfection.

Peter Elbow called this kind of writing *freewriting*. We are to write freely without stopping to correct, cross out, think, rethink, rephrase, edit,

---

89   *IZ Quotes*, s.v. Norbert Platt quote, izquotes.com/quote/302453. Note that many websites which offer the quotation I am referencing leave out the second *r* of Platt's first name. Information researchers with whom I have consulted believe that *Norbet* is a typographical error and that Norbert Platt, formerly of Montblanc International, is, indeed, the originator of the quotation as I have reported it.

or do anything to interfere with the flow of our feelings and thoughts. In his book *Writing Without Teachers*, Elbow observes:

> But it's not just "mistakes" or "bad writing" we edit as we write. We also edit unacceptable thoughts and feelings, as we do in speaking … Editing, in itself, is not the problem. Editing is usually necessary if we want to end up with something satisfactory. The problem is that editing goes on *at the same time* as producing … The habit of compulsive, premature editing doesn't just make writing hard. It also makes writing dead. Your voice is damped out by all the interruptions, changes, and hesitations between the consciousness and the page. [90]

If you find you are still someone who feels more comfortable composing on your computer, consider typing in a "freewriting" kind of way—let's call it *freetyping*. Just type away. Don't stop to correct typos, think, or edit.

I've found a small portable timer helpful. You can find one in your local kitchen store or in the kitchen section of your local department store. Alternatively, if you have a smartphone you can download any number of apps with timers and even choose your own chime.

To write with a timer is to follow in the tradition of Peter Elbow and Natalie Goldberg, author of *Writing Down the Bones*. *Timed writing* means exactly what you think it means. It means setting a timer for a set time before you begin to write, and writing without stopping until the timer sounds.

Setting a timer enables us to focus on our writing more intently, to use our writing time more efficiently, and to mitigate distraction.

---

90   Peter Elbow, *Writing Without Teachers* (New York: Oxford University Press, 1973), 5–6.

BE OPEN TO EMOTION

For many of us, generating material for a forever letter and writing a forever letter can be an emotional experience. We may find ourselves in tears. I mention this because if you feel uncomfortable crying in public, you may prefer to write at home.

As we write to our parents, grandparents, teachers, and mentors, we may find ourselves confronting their mortality. Who were these giants in our lives? Did they fulfill our expectations? What do we love about them? What do we admire about them? How did they fail us? How did they uplift us? What pieces of the past must we confront or surrender to move on with our lives?

As we write to our children, grandchildren, and students, we may find ourselves confronting *our* mortality, or at least I found this was true for me when I wrote to Gabriel. To write to him from the depths of my soul, to express my values and my love, to write what might be my last letter to him, I found myself imagining myself no longer living, no longer around to give guidance, to share my values and my love. I found myself imagining Gabriel continuing to live his life without me as an active participant. I found myself hoping for many more years of life, to watch him grow into a young man, to marry, and to have children; but I was also well aware of the fact that if this were not to be, he would at least have this letter (see appendix B).

There are other reasons that generating material for a forever letter can be an emotional experience. We face relationships that have soured. We face relationships we've nurtured and that have deepened beyond our expectations. We realize we aren't the people we thought we were. We realize we aren't as weak as we think. We realize we're actually quite wonderful despite our faults. We discover that we've never fully lived. We see how bitter we've become. We discover that as we've aged, we've gotten better at living. We're grateful to be alive. We feel blessed to have a loving family and loving friends. The list goes on.

In my workshops, I watch people as they write. I can't count the number of times I've seen a man's forehead furrow in deep concentration as his hand hurries across the page, a woman wipe away the tears that have begun to roll down her cheeks, a man grab a handful of tissues to dab his eyes before his tears fall, or a woman's lips quiver as she looks off into the distance. It's an intense and cathartic task, of contemplating our lives, the lives of the people we love, our relationships with them, and committing our thoughts to the page.

If tears of sadness or joy flow, let them flow. If tears happen to fall on your work, dab your work with a tissue and keep on writing. In the words of writer, essayist, and historian Washington Irving: "There is a sacredness in tears. They are not the mark of weakness, but of power. They speak more eloquently than ten thousand tongues. They are the messengers of overwhelming grief, of deep contrition, and of unspeakable love."[91] It's often from this place of emotion that deep writing is born.

SHOW UP

The first commitment you must make to yourself is to create time in your busy schedule to generate material for your forever letter, and then to write it. To begin, set a date. Set a time. Set aside two hours. And show up. If there's an emergency (illness, death of a loved one) that prevents

---

91   This quotation has been attributed to both Washington Irving and Samuel Johnson. For example, it was attributed to Washington Irving by Louis Klopsch in his *Many Thoughts of Many Minds* (2008), and again in *Dictionary of Quotations,* compiled by James Wood (London, New York: Frederick Warner & Co., 1899); and Bartleby .com (2012), www.bartleby.com/345/authors/258.html, which was my direct source. The same quotation was attributed to Samuel Johnson by Daniel B. Quinby, editor, in *Monthly Literary Miscellany, Vols. 6-7* (1852). Since my more contemporary sources attribute the quotation to Washington Irving, I am accepting Irving as author of that quotation for the purposes of this book.

you from showing up, reschedule your appointment with yourself. Annie Dillard understood the importance of showing up when she wrote in *The Writing Life*, "A schedule defends from chaos and whim. It is a net for catching days. It is a scaffolding on which a worker can stand and labor with both hands at sections of time." [92] Don't fool yourself by thinking: "I'll get to it eventually. I don't have to reschedule." You must reschedule. If you don't, you may not get to it.

I know about not getting to it. When I served as a full-time congregational rabbi, my schedule was filled with meetings, hospital visits, counseling, correspondence, preparing for classes, teaching, writing sermons, speaking, officiating at baby namings, bar and bat mitzvahs, weddings, and funerals. Weekdays. Weekends. Evenings. Don't get me wrong, I'm not complaining. I loved it, but I had a hard time in the midst of that schedule making time for myself.

I was blessed to have wonderful role models and mentors. One of them—I can't remember which one—advised me to guard my time. "Here's what you do," that person said. "Schedule appointments with yourself, appointments to swim, to meet a friend for lunch or dinner, to walk, to write. Put these appointments in your calendar. Honor them." Sounds simple, doesn't it? It wasn't as simple as it sounds. It took me many months to integrate this way of thinking into my being; but once I did, I became healthier, calmer, more productive, and a better listener and guide.

It's been nineteen years since I served as a full-time congregational rabbi. You'd think that I would have learned the art of making time for myself, but I had more to learn, especially when I married and had a child. For years I had a tendency to over-program myself and my family. Sometimes it was with people we wanted to see. Other times it was with events I felt we had to attend or invitations we owed. My husband helped me

---

92 Annie Dillard, *The Writing Life* (New York: Harper & Row, 1989), 32.

to see that in my desire to make space for everyone else, I left little time for each of us to accomplish what we needed to accomplish, and even less time for us to be together as a family. Though I'm getting better, to this day I'm still learning. I hope you're better at setting your priorities than I am. If you are, you're lucky. If you aren't, you're in good company. But let that good company go. Set time aside to generate material. Set aside time to write. Make writing your forever letters a priority.

Consider a Writing Partner

If you find the thought of generating material or writing a forever letter too difficult to contemplate doing on your own, or if you find yourself procrastinating, consider partnering with a friend.

The point of this partnership is to make the process of writing as supportive and as easy as possible. Choose someone you trust and respect, someone who will push you forward, and who will not compete with you. Choose someone with whom you feel safe.

You and your partner set the ground rules and decide how you want to work together. You have options. You can approach the writing partnership as you would a running, biking, or swimming partnership. You meet at a café, library, in each other's homes, and show up at a set time to keep each other on task. Or you can approach the writing partnership as you would a check-in call to a friend or family member to report arrival at your destination—your check-in call enables you to hold each other accountable. You can also approach the writing partnership by going on a retreat together to create the time and space to devote to this project.

8

WRITING PROMPTS

Fill your paper with the breathings of your heart.
—WILLIAM WORDSWORTH [93]

In this chapter I present three types of writing prompts to help you generate material for your forever letter: sentence completions, questions, and techniques for "stirring it up." I suggest beginning with the sentence completions; they are the most intimate way to access our inner selves because when we write down the beginning of a sentence that we are to complete, we immediately integrate this sentence into our narrative. Next, head to the questions because they are a little more cerebral. Regarding the techniques

---

93 William Wordsworth, qtd. in *The Letters of William and Dorothy Wordsworth VIII: A Supplement of New Letters*, Letter dated 29 April 1812, ed. Alan G. Hill (Oxford, United Kingdom: Clarendon Press, 1993), 51.

for stirring it up, I'd encourage you to save these for last since each is an exercise in itself and will take more time to complete.

All of these prompts are designed to mine the place where our deep material lies, to center us, ground us, take us deep into our emotions and memories, and invite us to think honestly about ourselves, the person to whom we're writing, and our relationship with that person.

You need not write to all the prompts; let them serve as a guide. If they're helpful, use them. If not, invent your own. You'll find some overlap between the prompts within each category and among the prompts from different categories. This is purposeful. I've found that a slight alteration in the way a prompt is phrased can spark a different response.

You'll notice that some of these prompts are geared toward self-reflection, others toward reflection on the person you're writing to, and others toward reflection on the relationship you share with that person. It's important that you write to prompts from each of these three categories. It's also important that you write to prompts that make you uncomfortable. When prompts make us uncomfortable, it's often a sign that this is where we must go.

Before you begin, decide to whom you'll be writing. Bring that person to mind. Imagine that person standing before you. Feel that person's presence. Choose a sentence completion. Write it down. Set a timer for three minutes.

In keeping with Peter Elbow and Natalie Goldberg, I encourage you to write without lifting your pen from the page, even if you feel stuck. Better to write, "I'm not sure what I want to say," over and over again than to write nothing. Eventually you will tire from writing this sentence, and you'll figure out something you do want to say, which will lead you to something else you want to say, until you're hardly aware that you're writing.

When the timer beeps, complete the sentence you're writing. If you have additional thoughts that you don't want to forget, jot yourself a few notes and leave an empty page in your notebook so you can return to add these thoughts at a later time.

Continue in this manner until you've completed twelve to fifteen sentences. When you finish, ask yourself these questions: Have I learned anything new about myself? Have I learned anything new about the person I'm writing to? Have I learned anything new about my relationship with this person? There's no need to write down your answers; just take them in and let them inform you.

Before you head back to your life, schedule your next appointment. Two to three writing appointments of two hours each should be enough time. Try to schedule your writing appointments as close together as possible to allow for continuity.

Type your work. Save it on the computer and print out a hard copy. Place this hard copy in a folder with a title of your choosing. The sentence completions, questions, and techniques for stirring it up that follow can also be found in appendix C for quick reference when you are ready to begin generating material for your forever letter.

Sentence Completions

1. The values I believe in are...

2. The values I believe in and find hard to live are...

3. Here's what I learned from my parents...

4. Here's what I wish I had learned from my parents...

5. Here's what I learned from my grandparents, grandchildren, sister(s), brother(s), children, teachers, students, aunts, uncles, mentors, friends (choose one for each three-minute write)...

6. The most important people in my life are/were...

7. The stories that have guided me in my life are...

8. The most meaningful lessons I have learned have been ...

9. My strengths as a person are ...

10. My strengths as a daughter (son), sister (brother), partner (spouse), wife (husband), mother (father), grandmother (grandfather), other family member or friend are ...

11. My weaknesses as a person are ...

12. My weaknesses as a daughter (son), sister (brother), partner (spouse), wife (husband), mother (father), grandmother (grandfather), other family member or friend are ...

13. The most powerful gift(s) I have to offer is (are) ...

14. The most powerful gift(s) I have received is (has been) ...

15. My personal challenges and struggles have been ...

16. I've lived up to my ideals by ...

17. I've fallen short of my ideals by ...

18. What I most want to tell the people I love about me ...

19. What I most want to tell the people I love about them ...

20. I love you because ...

21. These are your strengths ...

22. Here is what you have taught me ...

23. My hopes for you are ...

24. As I review my life, I regret ...

25. As I review my life, I'm grateful for ...

26. Please forgive me for ...

27. I forgive myself for ...

28. I'm trying to forgive myself for ...

29. I can't forgive myself for ...

30. I forgive you for ... [94]

31. What I most want to be remembered for ...

32. My blessings for you are ...

33. May you ...

QUESTIONS

1. Describe a time in your life when an important value was formed. Why is this value so important to you?

2. What is the most precious gift you have ever received? Was it an actual gift? Was it words? Was it an experience you shared with someone you love(d)? Why was this gift so meaningful?

3. What are your top ten values? Are you living these values? Why? Why not?

4. What organizations do you belong to? Why?

5. What organizations do you contribute to? Why?

6. Do the organizations you belong to and contribute to match your values?

7. What values do you want to share with the person(s) you're writing to?

---

94   This one entry in this list is from Jack Riemer and Nathaniel Stampfer, *So That Your Values Live On—Ethical Wills and How to Prepare Them* (Woodstock, Vermont: Jewish Lights Publishing, 2003), 231.

8. Who are (were) the ten most important people in your life? Why?

9. What are the ten most important causes in your life? Why?

10. What are the ten most important objects in your life? What does each represent? Did you acquire these objects on your own or were they given to you? By whom?

11. What words have helped you move forward in your life? What words have held you back? Who delivered these words?

12. What messages have your parents, children, grandparents, grandchildren, siblings, teachers, students, mentors, friends left you with?

13. What do you most want the recipient of your words to understand about you? How would knowing these things about you help your relationship?

14. Can you trace any of your values back to a certain moment in time? Do you recall when any of your values originated? Who helped to instill these values? How? Why?

15. If you died tomorrow, what would the people closest to you say about you?

16. In the novel *Demian: The Story of Emil Sinclair's Youth*, Hermann Hesse wrote: "If you hate a person, you hate something in him that is part of yourself. What isn't part of ourselves doesn't disturb us." [95] Even when we don't hate another, we can be bothered by things that person says or does. So try this. What bothers you about the person(s) you're writing to? Make a list. When you've completed that list, circle those words that bother you about

---

95   Herman Hesse, *Demian: The Story of Emil Sinclair's Youth* (Harper Perennial, Modern Classics 1999, reissued 2009), 97.

yourself. Ask yourself if there is any way you can be kinder toward and less judgmental of yourself. Can you carry this kindness over to the person(s) to whom you are writing?

17. Consider these words from the philosopher, poet, and political activist Abraham Joshua Heschel: "The problem we face, the problem I as a father face, is why my child should revere me. Unless my child will sense in my personal existence acts and attitudes that evoke reverence—the ability to delay satisfactions, to overcome prejudices, to sense the holy, to strive for the noble— why should she revere me?" [96] Then answer the question: What about me deserves the reverence of my child, grandchild, parent, grandparent, niece, nephew, uncle, aunt, teacher, student, friend?

TECHNIQUES FOR STIRRING IT UP

GENERATE A TIME LINE

Draw a horizontal line on a sheet of paper. This will be the time line of your life. Mark it with important milestones: the year you were born, the year you graduated from high school, college, graduate school, the year you were married, the year you adopted your child, the years your grandchildren were born.

Include defining moments. Defining moments are moments that change us, challenge us, or spark within us a new or increased awareness of ourselves, our relationships, or our world. Sometimes a defining moment is an event. Sometimes a defining moment is a realization that happens over time.

What are your defining moments? Think about the year you retired, divorced, or told your family you were gay; the year you got sober, switched

---

96 Abraham Joshua Heschel, *The Insecurity of Freedom* (New York: Farrar, Straus and Giroux, 1966), 39–40.

careers, or began therapy; the year you lost fifty pounds, got cancer, or went into remission. Maybe there's a particular day you want to acknowledge, the day you fell in love, found the job of your dreams, or the day your child first spoke. Maybe there's a whole period of time that you want to acknowledge: years of abuse or neglect, a year abroad, or a sabbatical year.

When you are finished, ask yourself what events or experiences you forgot or neglected to include. Did you include the birth of your siblings? Your pivotal friendships? Your relationships with mentors? Your jobs, awards, travel? Did you include the deaths of the people you loved? Did you include your spiritual life? Were there spiritual highs in your life that helped you move forward? Spiritual lows that took you down? Does this time line of your life give you any insight into yourself, your relationships with others, and specifically your relationship(s) with the person(s) to whom you're writing?

You can conclude this time line with the present moment or you can imagine your time line through the end of your life. How long do you live? What do you have yet to accomplish that you want to build into your time line?

WRITE YOUR EULOGY

Shirley told me that Irving, her eighty-seven-year-old brother, wrote his own eulogy. His decision came about after his daughter-in-law died of breast cancer and he felt that the eulogy delivered at her funeral didn't do her justice. Irving didn't want a eulogy delivered at his funeral that didn't do him justice, so he took matters into his own hands.

As a chaplain, I had a similar experience. Over a period of five years, I met regularly with Burt, a man in his mid-eighties. When Burt's health began to fail and he knew he was dying, he told me that he wanted me to officiate at his funeral, and he began to dictate what he wanted me to say. I took copious notes as he spoke about his life: his childhood; his work; his wife, the love of his life, who had died twelve years earlier; his family;

and his newborn great-granddaughter. In his desire to communicate his values, Burt said that he lived by the golden rule, that he never took advantage of anyone or intentionally mistreated anyone, that he employed kids from local schools part-time, gave them decent wages, and allowed the really good ones to work on commission to make more.

To write your eulogy is to explore even more deeply the essence of your life on this earth. Some pieces you see in yourself might delight you. Other pieces might disturb you. Maybe you'll see that you are already the person you want to be, or maybe you'll see that you're not yet the person you'd like to be. So, how do you accept who you are? Or how do you become the person you want to become?

WEAVE WORD WEBS

Weaving word webs can help to remind you of stories related to particular values. Choose a value that is important to you. Write that value in the center of a piece of white unlined paper. Circle it. Draw lines from this circle to an empty place on the page. Write a specific word that relates to this value. For example, I'm writing a forever letter to my son, Gabriel. I write the word *kindness* in the center of the page. I circle it. I ask myself what comes to mind? I write *purple elephant*. I draw a line from *kindness* to *purple elephant*. Why do I write down *purple elephant*? Because I remember the stuffed purple elephant that Gabriel loved when he was four, the elephant he carried with him everywhere, until he gave it away to a girl he did not know when he saw her crying. I then ask myself what other acts of kindness come to mind when I think about Gabriel. I write *playground*. I draw a line from *kindness* to *playground*. I write *Edith*, an elder friend in our community. I draw a line from *kindness* to *Edith*. I continue on until the page is full of lines and looks like a giant spiderweb.

COMPOSE A SONG

A first-generation Chinese-American man told me that when his father was living in China and wasn't sure if his health would allow him to make it to the United States, he wrote a song in Chinese that captured the values he wanted to pass on to his children. He taught that song to his wife and to his son. Consider writing your forever letter in verse, or consider writing a song to accompany it.

DRAW A PICTURE

This same Chinese-American man told me that when his mother was in the hospital and unable to speak, she drew a picture that resembled a tree. He asked her questions about that tree. Questions such as, "Mom, is this a tree? Are you drawing a tree because you want us to have children? To grow spiritually? To have deep roots?" In response to his questions, she would nod. It was through this drawing that she passed on her values. Consider drawing a picture to include in your forever letter.

CREATE AN EXPERIENTIAL FOREVER LETTER

There are several approaches you can take to creating an experiential forever letter. One is to take the recipient(s) of your forever letter on a trip that highlights some of the values you find meaningful. This was the approach taken by Menachem Daum, an Orthodox Jewish filmmaker and the son of Holocaust survivors. Daum was worried that his yeshiva-student sons were becoming so entrenched in their faith that they were becoming intolerant of others who did not share their beliefs. Seeking to encourage his sons to be more open-minded, Daum persuaded them to join him and his wife, Rivka, on a trip to Europe to return to the towns where his parents had been born and to find the Catholic family that had hidden Rivka's father and Rivka's father's two brothers. Their sons agreed but seemed to do so more out of respect for their parents than a desire to go. They seemed to have little investment in their journey—until they saw the remains of a synagogue destroyed by the Nazis and until they met Matuszezyk Mucha, the woman who had risked her life and her family's lives by hiding and feeding the boys' grandfather and their grandfather's two brothers during the war. Only after meeting her did these yeshiva students realize that without the kindness of this woman and her family, they would not be alive. Out of this experience Daum created the documentary *Hiding and Seeking*.[97]

Another approach to creating an experiential forever letter is to generate challenges for the person you're writing to, challenges that encourage this individual to discover or to develop his or her values. In the inspirational tale and subsequent motion picture *The Ultimate Gift*,[98] Jim Stovall tells the story of Jason Stevens, who stands to inherit billions of dollars from his great uncle Red's multibillion-dollar estate, but there's a catch. To receive this gift, Jason must prove worthy; to prove worthy, he must partake in a yearlong experience designed to develop values that in his entitled and privileged youth, he has not yet learned.

This yearlong experience is left in the hands of Ted Hamilton, his uncle Red's lawyer and best friend, at whose office Jason must appear each month to receive his monthly challenge (gift). Each month Ted Hamilton and his assistant, Miss Hastings, show Jason a prerecorded video by his uncle Red, who describes the challenge (gift) for that month and the assignment he's responsible for by month's end to show how he has come to understand that month's gift. Examples of these gifts include work, friends, giving, dreams, and laughter. If at the end of each month Jason's understanding of that gift meets Ted Hamilton's standards, Jason can proceed to the next month's gift and on to the ultimate gift; if not, the experience ends. For the first few

---

97   Oren Rudavsky and Manachem Daum, *Hiding and Seeking: Faith and Tolerance after the Holocaust,* (2004; San Francisco, CA: Independent Television Service, 2004), DVD.

98   Jim Stovall, *The Ultimate Gift* (Colorado Springs, CO: David C. Cook, 2007).

months, the entitled and privileged Jason shows up with an attitude, but the more he invests himself in the process, the more he begins to understand that these challenges are growing him into a more compassionate human being, and by year's end, he has lost his obsessive interest in the money he is to inherit.

Consider creating an experiential forever letter. The experience you create can involve travel, community service, or a series of challenges. It can take place after you have died, or while you are still alive—perhaps it's an experience that you and the person or people you're writing to take together.

Engrave a Forever Letter in Stone

Gladys, in her sixties, told me that she and her husband came up with the idea of using their gravestone as a way of imparting their values. At the bottom of their stone are the words, "That future generations may bless us for their past." On the left side of the stone are six boxes. Engraved into each box is a different scene that highlights their values. Included in these boxes: a Torah scroll, challah, a wine cup, family, books, writing paper and quill, a family tree, a hand inside a heart.

Contemplate engraving your values onto your gravestone. Or, try this: If you had only ten words or ten images to communicate what is most meaningful to you, what words and images would you choose?

9

WRITE AND EDIT YOUR FOREVER LETTER

*I write entirely to find out what I'm thinking, what I'm
looking at, what I see and what it means.
What I want and what I fear.*

—JOAN DIDION [99]

Among the topics this chapter speaks to are: the fears that sometimes emerge as we begin to write; the importance, when possible, of giving our words time to incubate; questions to consider as we review our letters and our prompts; suggestions for editing, presentation, and feedback; and the expectations we have when we decide to present our forever letters to the

---

99   Joan Didion, "Why I Write," *New York Times Book Review*, December 5, 1976.
      Adapted from a Regents Lecture delivered at the University of California, Berkeley.

people we love during our lives instead of leaving them to be found after we die.

LET GO OF FEAR AND WRITE

To write your forever letter, schedule a two-hour appointment with yourself (and with your writing partner if you're working with a partner), just as you did when you set time aside to generate material. Know that there are people who finish writing a forever letter in one sitting and feel it is complete, but that there are many (especially those writing more personal forever letters) who need to schedule another couple appointments with themselves to complete it.

Before you begin to write, take a few moments to contemplate the person (or persons) to whom you're writing. Consider this person's special qualities, the moments in this person's life that stand out. Remember shared experiences. Ask yourself, "What do I most want to say to this person?"

Let's say you're writing to your daughter. Consider writing about the time when she was four years old and kissed another toddler's knee at the playground after he had fallen. Or, say you're writing to your mentor and professor, consider mentioning how in awe you are of her cutting-edge discoveries in brain research and how you're looking forward to being her teaching assistant.

You can also write about moments when the person you're writing to fell short. You can write to your nephew about the night he went out drinking with his friends, got drunk, banged up the car, and almost killed himself to highlight some of the lessons he learned from that experience. You can write to your friend about the time she dated a handsome man who mistreated her and how it helped her to change her priorities from "looks are everything" to "character matters, too."

You can write about yourself and your values, about moments in your life when you faced difficult situations and behaved in ways you were proud of or in ways you regret. Such as: the time you pushed your way to the top of your company, stepping on everyone to get there, but how, when you got to the top, it took only six months before you were laid off because no one trusted you, and how it took a yearlong depression to get you in tune with your values.

You may want to have a visual, a photograph of the person to whom you're writing, to keep you company. Kate, in her forties, who had a loving yet difficult relationship with her mother, told me in a conversation unrelated to forever letters that on occasion she would talk to a photograph of her mother to give her the practice and strength she needed to be able to talk to her mother in person. As she spoke, I thought this would be a good idea for forever letter writers. Sometimes seeing the person we're writing to in a photograph can help us be more compassionate, can give us the strength we need to write, or can serve as inspiration. Additional inspiration might come from placing next to that photograph a meaningful item that person has given you.

Settle in.

As you write, push aside your internal editor, that critical voice within you that holds you back, that says, "I could have said that better," or "This is not the right word," or "I'm being too severe," or "I can't tell her what I really think," or "What would she think if she read this line?" Be with whatever comes up—the sadness, the joy, the anger, the delight, the hurt, the gratitude, the disappointment, the love. Don't worry about what you write. You need not show a single soul your work. This is a draft. You'll have the opportunity to craft and edit later.

In her book *Bird by Bird: Some Instructions on Writing and Life*, the author Anne Lamott writes about "shitty first drafts" and the dangers of perfectionism: "Perfectionism is the voice of the oppressor, the enemy of the people. It will keep you cramped and insane your whole life, and it is the main obstacle between you and a shitty first draft … Besides, perfectionism will ruin your writing, blocking inventiveness and playfulness and life force…Perfectionism means that you try desperately not to leave so much mess to clean up. But clutter and mess show us that life is being lived." [100]

If panic ensues because you're not sure what you most want to say, or because you find yourself engaged in self-doubt, wondering how you can talk about what is most meaningful to you when you've made so many mistakes of your own, acknowledge these feelings. Take a few deep breaths. Let these feelings go. You've already done a series of exercises to prepare yourself to write. Trust that you're ready, that you have something to say, and that the person you're writing to wants to hear what you have to say.

Your forever letter can be long or short, general or personal. It can be written as a stand-alone letter or combined with a family history, but don't worry about any of this before you begin to write. Just write. The emerging material will help you decide how it wants to be crafted.

Begin by writing the word *Dear,* and the name(s) of the person(s) to whom you're writing.

Start writing.

Keep writing.

When you are done, type it up and put it in the same folder with your prompts. You'll return to all the material you've generated during the editing process.

OUR WORDS NEED TIME TO INCUBATE

I've found great value in suggesting, when possible, a wait of at least one month before returning to your file of prompts and to the forever letter you've written. I suggest this for a few reasons. When we write, we discover or rediscover things about ourselves, about the person we're writing to, and about our relationship with that person. These discoveries take

---

100 Anne Lamott, *Bird by Bird: Some Instructions on Writing and Life* (New York: Anchor Books, 1995), 22, 28.

time to process. Letting this process mill around inside us without paying conscious attention to it, we grow.

Sometimes during this month new ideas will hatch, ideas we may want to include in our final draft: ideas about ourselves, the other, our shared relationship. These ideas come at all hours of the day and night, and when they come, I encourage you to write them down on pieces of paper and drop them into your folder. These ideas come because we've opened up the space in our minds, hearts, and souls to be receptive to them.

When we return to our prompts and our forever letters after having let them incubate, we often find we have fresh eyes for what we've written and are better able to determine if our words communicate what we intend for them to communicate.

There are times when an incubation period isn't possible, however. Those suffering from illnesses often don't have the luxury of time. In these situations, sometimes it's more important to get our thoughts onto the page than it is to get our words exactly right.

I learned this from Ann in April 2013, when I received the letter below.

Dear Rabbi Zaiman,

I am writing to you with my thank you story: In December of 2009, my husband Sheldon was diagnosed with an aggressive brain tumor when he was 55 years old. [At the time you offered your workshop], Sheldon had completed a craniotomy, radiation, and chemotherapy. He attended your workshop and enjoyed it very much, especially the opportunity to begin writing his own [forever letter]. That afternoon, he wrote out short sentences and phrases to answer some of the open-ended questions on your handout. He was convinced that he would finish it on his own. He wrote notes on a legal yellow pad inside a leather portfolio and put it aside on his desk.

During the two years that followed, Sheldon's condition had its ups and downs. He would have another craniotomy, attempts at three different types of treatments and a few hospitalizations. He lost part of his visual field and suffered from other cognitive issues that would be expected with a brain tumor. By the summer of 2012, he was steadily declining and under in-home hospice care. In early fall, I started to look through the accumulated papers on Sheldon's desk, searching for important documents and trying to make order. I found the portfolio and, for the first time, saw the notes that he had written for his [forever letter]. I typed the notes up and then took the document to him. I tried to ask him to clarify some of the phrases and notes he had written nearly two years before. By that time, it was difficult for him to remember what he meant, but he was able to clarify a few of his notes. We got interrupted by a visitor, so I put the document aside. As it turned out, that day was the last time Sheldon got out of bed, and his decline accelerated. We were never able to return to the questions about his [forever letter].

Sheldon was a *baal koreh* [Torah reader, one who reads the biblical text from the scroll itself] from the time of his bar mitzvah reading almost weekly for many years. When [the holiday of] *Simchat Torah* came, Sheldon was in bed, barely communicating. We had someone that Sheldon mentored come to the house that night and read the end of *Devarim* [Deuteronomy] to Sheldon and our gathered family. After hearing Moshe's [Moses's] last words to his people, and knowing that even Moshe could not fulfill his life's dream of bringing the nation into its land, I asked Sheldon if he would give me permission to read the [forever letter] to our three children. So I read it to them in the presence of their dying father. In it,

Sheldon stated his values of education, hard work, Israel and family. Everyone who knew Sheldon knew those things because he was a man who lived out his values. He wrote of some of the things that he was sorry about and of things he regretted not doing, and he forgave us. What was written was short— less than two typed pages, with sections that were "notes" and whose meaning remains unclear to us. The result, however, was important. Our children felt like their father had personally said things to them that they had waited to hear. In the short sentences, he commented on aspects of their relationship of which they did not think he was aware. Those phrases and sentences brought a sense of peace and closure to all of them. In the days that followed, Sheldon became less and less able to interact with this world and he died less than two weeks later. That [forever letter] will remain with our children—both in printed form and in their hearts.

And so, I wanted to thank you for this important gift you gave our family. I hope your workshops continue to inspire other people to leave this gift to their family. A life is never finished, and even an unfinished [forever letter] reflects the gift that that life brought us.

With sincere appreciation,
Ann [101]

EDIT: REREAD, REWRITE, REREAD (2x)

Return to your folder. Reread your forever letter, your prompts, and any notes you placed into your folder. If you find material in your prompts

---

101   Brackets and italics are mine. Brackets indicate explanation. Brackets around forever letter indicate my change of *ethical will* to *forever letter*.

or in your notes that you want to include in your forever letter, now's the time to work this material in. If new thoughts come to you, add them in. Then ask yourself the questions below. These questions can be found in appendix C for quick reference when you are ready to begin to edit your forever letter.

1. Does my forever letter sound like me?

2. Does it communicate my essence?

3. Am I present to the person I'm writing to, meeting that person where he or she is, in a way he or she can hear?

4. Have I been open and vulnerable, sharing personal experiences?

5. Have I asked for forgiveness? Have I forgiven?

6. If I have stated hard truths, have I done so with love?

7. Have I avoided commanding with the pen?

8. Have I honored the strengths of the person I'm writing to?

9. Have I expressed my love, gratitude, and belief in the person(s) I'm writing to?

10. Are these the words by which I want to be remembered?

After you've answered the questions above and reworked your forever letter to your satisfaction, do some basic editing. Check for typos, clarity of thought, word choice, and consistency. Are there uncomfortable silences you must address, half-baked thoughts longing for fuller expression, hidden emotions bubbling beneath the surface?

When you feel finished, read your letter out loud. My hope is that you will consider reading it out loud two times, once from your point of view as the author and once from the point of view of the person you're writing to. There's something about hearing our words out loud from these two perspectives that helps us to better clarify our intent. It's not my desire to burden you with these two approaches. My desire is only to enable you to gain deeper insight into your words.

Say a nephew is writing to his aunt. When he reads his forever letter out loud the first time, from his point of view as the author, he can ask himself if he has said all he wants to say in the way he wants to say it. When he reads it out loud the second time, from the point of view of his aunt, he can imagine himself in his aunt's place, reading his words, and he can ask himself if he feels he's done right by her.

Reading out loud from these two points of view enables us to edit our words with deeper love and understanding.

SEEK FEEDBACK

There will be many of you who will not feel the need to seek feedback from others because you feel confident in your creation. If, however, you are worried about tone or about coming across as distant, condescending, judgmental, critical, false, sentimental, or sappy, now's the time to seek feedback from a trusted friend, therapist, rabbi, priest, minister, imam, or elder.

Not everyone knows how to offer feedback. To offer honest and generous feedback takes time and energy. A gifted critiquer will be someone who honors your voice and who does not try to convert your voice into his or her own. A gifted critiquer will also be someone whose ego is not bound up with your accepting his or her suggestions.

Even the best critiquers can have their own agenda of which they remain unaware, especially in response to ethical issues. Some critiquers will be overly moralistic and others perhaps not moralistic enough. Take in the feedback you are offered. Sit with it for a few days. Consult your heart before you decide to accept or reject it. This is your letter, not the critiquer's. You know the person(s) you're writing to, and you have to trust that knowledge. The final decision about what edits to make rests with you.

PRESENTATION

There's something about handwriting that provides an immediate connection to the person who's writing to us, even before we read that person's words.

When I think about the handwritten letters I've received over the years, I remember letters from my great-grandma Ethel. We weren't blood-related; she became my great-grandmother by marriage. I didn't see her all that much, as she and my great-grandfather lived in Wisconsin and we lived in Rhode Island, but I remember her white beauty-parlor-puffed hair and her soft, fleshy upper arms, and I remember her flowery calligraphic script. She didn't write to me often but when she did, I saved not only her letter but the envelope in which it had arrived because her beautiful script made me feel as if I were a dignitary receiving an invitation to a ball, wedding, or state affair.

We can handwrite or type (especially if we have horrible handwriting) our forever letters. But because handwritten communication provides yet another connection to us, even when we decide to type our words, we may want to consider handwriting a few lines at the end to add a personal touch.

PATIENCE

Gabriel heard the forever letter that I wrote to him when he was six and a half. I believe he heard it. I quoted much of it in a High Holiday sermon, but I doubt he remembers it, even if he fully understood it at the time. My hope was to print it out as a stand-alone letter and hand it to him when he became a teenager. One day, when he was twelve and I was talking to him about the forever letter I had written to him, I pulled out a draft of this book and opened it to this letter, much the same way my father had handed me his letter, as part of a larger document, and said, "Here it is; you can read it." He started reading but, after working his way through the first two pages, asked if he could finish later. "Sure," I said. "Whenever you want." He has not yet asked to see it again. He's not a big reader. He does not like to spend time reading long letters. Am I disappointed? A little. But I understand. He'll read it when he's ready. I hope that day will come while I'm still living so that we can use it to jump-start further conversations, but I will not push him. He'll get to that letter in his own time.

I mention this experience with Gabriel because after we hand or mail our letter to the person for whom it is intended, we expect, crave, or even feel entitled to a response. After all, we've spent hours, days, sometimes even months, writing, thinking, crafting, revising, and editing. We've poured our heart and soul onto the page. The least the recipient(s) of our letters can do is to acknowledge our gift.

We must temper our need for immediate gratification and remind ourselves that we wrote this letter because we wanted to write it. It doesn't mean that our loved one is ready to read it. Nor, for that matter, does it mean that our loved one is ready to respond, even if he or she has read it. We may receive a response; we may not. And if we do, it may be a very different response than the one we had imagined.

Here's my suggestion: let time pass. If you receive a response and it's not the response you hoped for, sit with that response for a while and take it in. Perhaps it can inform you how to work on that particular relationship. If you do not receive a response after what you consider a substantial period of time, and you feel you need one, you can always reach out to your loved one, ask if your letter was received (if you mailed it) and if he or she has any thoughts to share.

I remember the day my father handed me that booklet of ethical wills and challenged me to figure out which one was his. What I can't remember is what I said to my father after I read his words. Did I seek him out to thank him? Or did I keep my tears to myself? Had he seen my red eyes and tear-stained face, he would have known how much his words meant to me, but I'm not sure I allowed myself to be seen. My point: lack of response might not mean lack of appreciation.

Sylvia, in her eighties, wrote heartfelt forever letters to her five children. We sat together one day as she spoke about writing these letters. She said that, though she had written these letters by hand, she had asked someone to type them as her hand was unsteady and her script hard to read, and that, though she had written about some hard topics, she had spent most of her time writing about her love and appreciation for her children. After she mailed her letters, she said she only heard back from her son who wanted to know who typed the letter. I asked her if she was disappointed by the lack of response. Sylvia said that she was. She felt that even if all her kids did was give her a hug when they saw her, it would have been enough.

As we sat together, we spoke of others things. Toward the end of our visit, Sylvia had a realization. She said that she was guilty of the same thing. She said that her father had once written her a letter, similar to the letters she had written to children, and that she had never responded.

"Why not?" I asked.

She smiled and said something to the effect of: Because it somehow felt complete.

CONCLUSION

Dear Reader,

We write forever letters with the hope that they will be as meaningful to those we address as they are for us to write. Whether our recipients decide to save our letters is their decision, but by writing, by going deep within and looking honestly at ourselves, our lives, and our relationships, we grow and change. Writing a forever letter can have a profound effect on how we live our lives, how we see ourselves, and how we heal our relationships. So what are you waiting for? Pick up your pen and take the plunge.

Blessings,
Elana

P.S. Consider keeping copies of the forever letters you write so you can return to them to remind you of who you were and who the person you were writing to was at the time you wrote.

P.P.S. Enjoy the process.

Appendix A: A Brief History of the Ethical Will

The ethical will, which focuses primarily on parents writing to their children, serves as the foundation for the forever letter, which broadens the topic to include other relationships. In this appendix, I present excerpts and summaries of ethical wills from the 1000s to the 1800s to give you deeper insight into this genre.

Topics covered in ethical wills include ritual advice on the laws of family purity, the Sabbath, charity, prayer, Torah study, fulfilling God's commandments, and burial instructions, as well as ethical advice on friendship, marriage, child-rearing, humility, gratitude, honoring the poor, forgiveness, honesty, visiting the sick, guarding against gluttony, anger, envy, hate, drunkenness, stinginess, excessive speech, gossip, lying, and impure fantasies. Health, diet, penmanship, grammar, and superstition are among some of the other topics mentioned—essentially, whatever was meaningful to the author was fair game. That all letters contained quotes from biblical and rabbinic texts is no surprise. Traditional texts encompassed the values that grounded, guided, and instructed these fathers in their everyday lives in the synagogue, study house, marketplace, and home.

One of the earliest ethical wills is believed to have been written by Eleazar the Great (Eleazar ben Isaac of Worms) to his son, and to date back to the mid-eleventh century (though scholars disagree). Here are some of his thoughts:

> My son! When you are aroused from your sleep at midnight, engage with your wife in holiness. Do not desecrate your mouth, even in playful jesting. It is certain that you will be held fully accountable for every exchange between you and your wife.
>
> Be most careful to cleanse your body and to build a place for your soul that she may remain beloved and dear.
>
> Be careful to visit the sick, because the visitor diminishes the illness and lightens the burden.
>
> Be trustworthy with every person. Do not reveal a person's secret when you have a dispute with him.
>
> Do not eat meat that is still steaming whether broiled or boiled. And do not eat food cooked in a pan that has not been cooked in for thirty days. [102]

Another early ethical treatise often placed in the category of the ethical will is titled "The Rule." It was written by Asher ben Yehiel, a rabbi and an authority on Jewish law, who lived from 1250 to 1327. In "The Rule," Asher ben Yehiel offered the community 131 rules for ethical conduct. Among them:

---

102   Israel Abrahams, *Hebrew Ethical Wills,* trans. Rabbi Dr. Moshe Shualy (unpublished, 2014), 36, 37, 40, 44, 49.

Be reluctant to engage in disputes.

Do not embarrass your fellow in public.

Do not hold back from acquiring a trusted friend. Protect him and watch over him. Do not lose him because therein is goodness.

Do not hold your anger against your friend for a single day. Humble yourself before him to ask his forgiveness.

Pave a path of righteousness in the middle road in eating and drinking.

Do not be compelled to find out the secrets among other persons. [103]

It's a few centuries later before we hear the voice of Glückel of Hameln, a mother and businesswoman, who lived from 1646 to 1724. To calm her grieving soul after the death of her first husband, Glückel wrote a memoir for her twelve children that is often quoted in the genre of ethical wills. She began her memoir by stating that her intention was not to offer a book of morals; yet, within her 277 pages, she, too, felt the need to offer ethical guidance, such as:

The best thing for you, my children, is to serve God from your heart, without falsehood or sham, not giving out to people that you are one thing while, God forbid, in your heart you are another.

Above all, my children, be honest in money matters, with both Jews and Gentiles, lest the name of Heaven be profaned. If you have in hand money or goods belonging to other people, give more care to them than if they were your own, so that, please God, you do no one a wrong. [104]

---

103 Abrahams, trans. by Rabbi Dr. Moshe Shulay, 119, 121, 122.

104 Glückel of Hameln, *The Memoirs of Glückel of Hameln* (New York: Schocken Books, 1977), 2–4.

I would not be doing justice to the genre of ethical wills if I didn't introduce you to ethical wills that admonish. Judah Ibn Tibbon's ethical will to his only son Samuel is an example of one such ethical will. Born in Granada in 1120 and forced to leave Spain in the mid-1100s, Ibn Tibbon established himself as a respected physician, scholar, translator, and book collector in Lunel, France, by 1160.

In his ethical will to Samuel (revised several times during his life) Ibn Tibbon did not hold back from admonishment. No topic was off limits. Among the topics he commented on: diet, dissatisfaction with his son's business practices (primarily because he was not consulted), marital advice, instructions on maintaining ongoing relationships with his sisters, and education.

Ibn Tibbon had a lot to say about education. He wrote about how he traveled long distances to secure Samuel a teacher in the secular sciences and how he went to great lengths to pay for Samuel's teachers and books. It's clear he was frustrated with Samuel—he lamented how his efforts were for naught, since Samuel never applied himself to his learning and showed himself to be lazy. Ibn Tibbon did not hide his disappointment:

> And you my son! You have disappointed my objectives and
> hopes. And you did not choose to utilize your wisdom. And
> you have ignored all your books (and their teachings). You had
> no interest in even seeing them or their titles. If you were to see
> them in the hands of others, you would not recognize them.
> And if you needed one of them, you would not know if you
> owned it or not, until you'd ask me ...
>
> Even Arabic writing which you started to learn seven years
> ago, and still I tried to appease you regarding mastering this
> great skill, and you refused to listen to me ...

Even regarding Hebrew writing you were not properly
observant. You well remember that proud scholar Rabbi Jacob, the
son of the gentleman Rabbi Obadiah, to whom I paid thirty gold
dinars every year. And when I pleaded with him to teach you to
write the letters, he said to me, "It's enough if he learns one letter
a year." And if your heart but aspired to his teaching, you would
have aspired to be a greater scribe than he or his sons. [105]

Ibn Tibbon's admonishment is harsh, even controlling, and probably
not the approach many of us would take were we writing to our children
today, but it's clear he felt that Samuel was capable of more and that he
wanted Samuel to utilize the intellectual gifts with which he had been
blessed. This is evident to me in the gentler tone he used in other parts of
his ethical will to encourage Samuel to befriend his books and to delight
in their knowledge, to study medical texts and to care for all who are sick,
even if they couldn't afford to pay, to prescribe only the drugs and herbs he
knew to be beneficial, to blind himself to the faults of others, but to recognize and understand his own faults. He also waxed on about Samuel's wise
and discerning heart, strong intellect, ease with language, and expertise in
matters of grammar and style. So impressed was he with his son's strengths
in these areas, he mentioned how even he had sought his son's guidance.

Another ethical will that admonished is that of Mordechai Mottel
Michelsohn (1800–1872). A learned man and community leader in the
Polish city of Kaluszyn, Michelsohn wrote to his sons toward the end of
his life, and was thus able to reflect on the entirety of his life: his difficult
childhood, his troubled life in communal politics, his sons' behaviors, and
his own behaviors. He was a man on a mission not only to guide his sons,
but to perfect his soul by stating his ultimate truth.

---

105 Abrahams, trans. by Rabbi Dr. Moshe Shulay, 57–60.

Michelsohn urged his sons to avoid behaviors like "stinginess and miserliness," "drunkenness and lying" as "they are despicable." He asked that their speech "be tempered, moderate, and concise because 'excessive speech, both in content and volume, adds abuse and crime'(Proverbs 10:19)." [106]

Harsh words, yes, and probably not words many of us would choose today, but Michelsohn did not just admonish his sons and leave it at that. Michelsohn shared a personal experience about a time his teacher admonished him. He wrote that he "failed," when he "intervened in a community matter, interjecting with a loud and forceful voice," and was advised by his teacher that "the sages communicate effectively by speaking gently, with restraint and pleasing moderation (reference to Ecclesiastes 9:17)." [107]

Toward the end of his ethical will, Michelsohn made it clear that his sons' behavior hurt him: "And now, my children, listen to your father's advice: Know that you have been contrary since the day we met. You neither listened nor remembered the good I did for you! Your behavior and business practices have caused me anger, sorrow, and pain. You despise me. Furthermore, none of my paths are followed." [108]

Harsh words again, and troubling to read, but after writing these words Michelsohn once again turned inward. He seemed to understand that just as his sons needed to be forgiven their wrongs, he, too, needed to be forgiven his wrongs, "But how may I chastise your violence, since we all have sinned? We are God's children … And though we sinned, God in His great mercies continues to love us, forgive us, and bestow good upon us. And I, who am human, not divine, forgive you, just as God forgives you for all manner of hidden sins." [109]

---

106 Mordechai Mottel Michelsohn, "The Ethical Will of Mordechai Mottel Michelsohn" in *Sefer Beit Meshulam*, trans. Rabbi Dr. Moshe Shualy and Mordechai Shualy (unpublished, 2016), 74, 75.

107 Ibid., 74, 75.

108 Ibid., 76.

109 Ibid., 76.

As I read these words, I'll admit that I found myself wishing Michelsohn had taken it one step further and had asked his sons for their forgiveness, but from the text it's clear that what mattered to him most was that they all be forgiven by God.

Wanting to conclude this appendix on a more uplifting note, I introduce you to one final ethical will. It was written by Alexander, son of Moses Suesskind, toward the end of his life, and published in 1794, the year he died. Alexander's ethical will speaks to his personal relationship with God, his hope of pleasing God, and his hope that his children live lives that please God. [110]

Alexander begins his ethical will with the words, "My children, whom I love," [111] and he returns to this sentiment many times. Even in this more loving tone, Alexander commands his children to follow his words and to pass his words onto their children. Absent from his ethical will, however, are words that admonish his children for not behaving in an ethical manner or in a manner of which he disapproved. Alexander focuses on himself and the improvements he needs to make in his life to improve his relationship to his Creator. Only after using himself as an example does he command his children to think of their behaviors in these same areas, and to ask themselves if their behaviors are pleasing to God.

Having written a well-received book on prayer for the community, Alexander, in his ethical will, also writes about prayer, and includes some of his personal prayers. Here are a few: a prayer requesting that no one intrude on him during prayer to cause him to interrupt his time with his Creator; a prayer thanking God for any bad that befalls him, because it enables him to see his own failings, and a prayer thanking God for the correspondence he receives from his children.

---

110   Excerpts of this ethical will can be found in Israel Abrahams, *Hebrew Ethical Wills* (Philadelphia: The Jewish Publication Society, 2006), 327–341.

111   Israel Abrahams, *Hebrew Ethical Wills*, trans. Elana Zaiman (unpublished, 2015), 328.

It's fascinating to read these ethical wills to get a sense of the different authors, the historical period during which each author lived, and, in the more personal ethical wills, to get a sense of the relationship these authors with their children.

Appendix B: A Forever Letter to My Son

I was forty-four when I wrote this, my first forever letter, to my son. He was six and a half. I began to cry shortly after writing the words, "Dear Gabriel." I'm a crier, so this wasn't surprising to me. But from the moment I wrote his name on the page, I became aware of how much I loved him, how much I hoped for him, and how much I wanted to be around to see him grow up.

As I wrote, specific memories came to mind, memories of my childhood with my parents, memories of Gabriel as an infant and a toddler, and memories of myself as a new mother. I remembered times when I had succeeded as a mother and times I had failed. I wrote it all down. I wasn't sure what would end up in my letter; I just knew I needed to write it.

I include excerpts from this letter here so that you can see what was most important to me at the time I wrote, some of the hard places I encountered, some of the lessons I learned, and some of the joys I experienced. Since writing this letter, I have written a few other forever letters to Gabriel. The letters I'm thinking of are not just everyday letters, but letters sharing love, guidance, and lessons learned that pertained to my understanding of myself, my childhood, my role as a mother, and my understanding of my son.

Someday, perhaps, when Gabriel gets married or has his first child, I will place this forever letter, other forever letters I have written, and still other forever letters I am bound to write into a three-ring binder, and hand this over to him as a reminder of who he was at a given point in time, who I was at a given point in time, how we each have grown, and how our relationship has unfolded.

Dear Gabriel,

I have wanted to write a forever letter to you for some time. But each time I start to write, I come up with excuses as to why I should wait. You're only six and a half. I'll have more to say to you when you're older, when I see who you are on the road to becoming. I'm only forty-four. Certainly, I'll have many more years to write to you. Truth is, these excuses are just that—excuses. I don't know how much time I have left in this world. And I do have a glimpse of who you are on the road to becoming.

The real reason I haven't written a forever letter to you is because it's hard. It's hard to imagine myself no longer living, no longer part of your life. In order to write you this letter that's what I must imagine. Even if you read my forever letter when I'm still alive. Say, when you are fourteen, the age I was when my father handed me a copy of his forever letter.

What lasting words do I want to leave you with? What do I want to tell you about me? About the Jewish values I learned as a child? About the Jewish values I have come to appreciate as an adult? What Jewish values do I want to pass on to you?

I must begin at the moment of our bonding, shortly after you entered this world. We were still in the hospital. I think it was the afternoon of the day you were born. The lactation consultant paid us a visit to teach me how to feed you.

We had trouble. We were both new at this. You had trouble latching on. I had trouble latching you on. We tried and tried. We tried again. Finally, you lost it.

You cried and cried. You wouldn't stop crying. I held you. I comforted you. I spoke to you, as if you could understand my words: "Gabriel, I'm trying so hard to feed you. I've never been a Mom before. I've never breast-fed before. I'm doing the best I can." You continued to cry. So I did the only thing I could. I cried, too.

And you know what you did? You stopped crying immediately. You stared at me with your big blue eyes. You seemed to understand that I was doing all I could to help you. Okay, maybe I'm reading into this look of yours, giving you credit for a compassion you did not know, understand, or intend, but to this day, watching your compassion toward others is one of my deepest joys.

Ever since you were a baby, I have tried to teach you compassion toward others, loving kindness, by modeling behaviors and actions I hoped you would emulate. Like visiting the elderly. Reaching out to those in need. Talking to children. Always talking to children who are physically handicapped. I want these children to feel good about themselves, good about being in this world. I want them to see that not everyone stares at them and turns away.

It was toward the end of December when you were three and a half. I was thinking a lot about my brother Rafi, who died. I was thinking of him, in part, because I was writing a story about him and in part because it was on December 31st twenty-four years earlier that he had been diagnosed with a tumor on the base of his spine. I was sad and in need of alone time, so you and your Dad went on an outing, while I stayed home and wrote.

"Mama, are you okay?" you asked when you came home and saw that my eyes were red from crying. "Yes, honey, I'm okay," I said. "I just miss Rafi. At this time of year, I think about him lots." "Mama, you stay right here. I be back. I be back," you said. "I make you better. I bring you Rafi." And off you ran down the hall and up the stairs, the whole way calling, "Mama, I help you. I help you."

I remember wondering what you were up to, wondering how you could bring me Rafi, if Rafi had died, but you finally returned, and you handed me Rafi's stuffed Snoopy. "Mama. I brought you Rafi. Now you feel better?"

I hugged Snoopy. I said, "Gabriel, thank you. You brought me Rafi's Snoopy. That's the closest thing to Rafi you could bring me." I asked you for a hug. When you hugged me, I cried again. This time, I cried because of your compassion.

When you were almost six, we took Edith, our eighty-year-old family friend, out to dinner. When we brought her home, we sat in her living room for a while. Knowing her husband had died three years earlier, you asked her if she was lonely living by herself. She said, "Yes, sometimes I am." And you said; "Edith when you're lonely, you should come over and sleep at our house, so you're not alone." You moved Edith to tears. It's not easy to move Edith to tears. I could go on and on with examples of your compassion. But you get the point. I don't know what you have picked up from me, from your father, or from others, and what is innately you. But I hope you continue in your care and concern for others, and let it always be from your heart.

Your ability to have compassion for others, to love others as yourself (Leviticus 19:18), has to do not only with your father and I modeling this behavior for you, and not only with your nature but with the love with which you have been loved. Loved by your parents, your grandparents, your aunts, uncles, cousins, and friends. From being loved, you have so much love inside you to give others. And you do give it. I am told you raise your hand in your class and say things like, "I like first-grade," and "MaryAnn, you are a great teacher." I watch you spontaneously hug and kiss the people you appreciate.

I believe you know that you are loved. Your father and I tell you how much we love you all the time. So much so that a few times you have told me in your adamant way, "Mama, I know. You tell me all the time." Not only do we tell you. We show you. We hug and we kiss you. We talk to each other in loving ways (usually). We're there for each other when we are sad. When someone dies. When something isn't going right. When one of us has a disagreement with a friend. We're there for each other when we are happy. Birthdays. Starting first grade. A new job. An article published.

Love. I can love you because I, too, was loved by my parents, grandparents, aunts, uncles, and cousins. My mother. Her love for me was constant and total. No matter what I did. No matter how I felt about myself. Her love was, and is, ever-present. "I will be with you," said God to Moses at the burning bush. I will accompany you on your way. You will never be alone. My mother saw us out the door in the morning on our way to school, and she welcomed us home in the afternoon. Even when I was at school, when she was not physically present, I knew she was always around. Her ever-present-ness gave me a sense of security to face challenges in the larger world. Even though I am home less for you than my mother was for me, I hope I have created such a foundation for you, a home, a place of comfort, a safe haven from which to move forward.

To this day, I call my mother when I'm sick. I'm not sure what she can do, living as she does on the other side of the country. But sometimes I just need to tell her how miserable I feel, and hear her say, "I'm sorry you're not feeling well." Her words, even from far away, help me heal.

I wonder how to teach you faith? I think back to my growing up. How did I become a person of faith?

Growing up, we talked about Judaism, about Torah, about ritual observance. We didn't talk about God. It wasn't like, hey, there's a God you need to believe. It was more like, we believe because we act: We engage in rituals, we study, we sing Hebrew melodies, we attend a Jewish Day School and Jewish summer camps. These actions speak to our belief.

As a child, I went to synagogue. I didn't have much of a choice. My father was the rabbi. The four of us kids were expected to be there. But synagogue didn't feel imposed. Synagogue inspired my faith, because I was in awe of my father, the rabbi, in awe of his majesty on the *bimah* [pulpit]. (About being a rabbi's child I will write you another letter, a different kind of letter.) I was in awe of the cantor, his inspiring voice, in awe of the liturgical melodies. Because of this, I felt a sense of holiness in my life, and I have no doubt that this sense of holiness influenced my faith.

Your father and I have provided you with all of that. Well, almost all of it. We go to synagogue, though not as often as I used to go when I was a girl. I find attending synagogue harder as I get older. I find I attend more for a sense of community than a sense of awe and spiritual connection. As of late, I have found in study, solitary prayer, and writing more of that spiritual connection.

Yes, we go to synagogue. Yes, we live a Jewish life. Yes, you attend a Jewish day school, and when you are old enough, you will attend a Jewish summer camp.

Is that enough? Maybe. I don't know. I have the sense that the roots of my faith go back to experiences in my childhood, experiences I don't even remember, but experiences I am reminded of often.

God called Abraham. (Abram at the time.) God said, essentially. Go forth on your journey. (Genesis 12:1). And Abram did. I, too, was called. Not by God initially, but by my father, the rabbi. The story goes that when I was three I would sit on his lap and he would ask me questions. Questions like: When you grow up, will you study Torah? Will you be a *mensch*? Will you live as a Jew? The incentive was the popsicle we were sharing. I'm told that if I answered yes, my father gave me a lick. And so I was called to follow the Jewish faith.

We had similar conversations when you were younger. Not with popsicles, but I would ask you questions like my father had asked me. Will you study Torah? Will you live a Jewish life? Will you do acts of loving-kindness? You would nod.

When you were around thirteen months, I sat you in front of a large tractate of the Talmud, and asked your Dad to take your picture. I thought *Zayde* and Grammy would get a kick out of our budding Talmud scholar, who could not yet read, much less speak. I thought in years to come you, too, would love to see yourself with a tractate of Talmud larger than you were. But I really took that picture for me, a dream, a hope, that Judaism will remain alive for you throughout the course of your life.

Other experiences I had as a child also contributed to my developing faith. Most mornings my mother woke us up for school. But on days she was downstairs making us breakfast, or preparing our lunches, the task of waking us up fell upon my father, who would walk into our room in his white boxer shorts and white undershirt and sing in a loud cantorial-like chant. "*Shtet uf lavoydes haboyreh.*" "Awake to worship the Lord." Though at the time I did not understand the meaning of this Hebrew chant, I understood that waking to a new day was a holy sacred task.

I taught you this chant at a young age. You even surprised *Zayde* and Grammy with it on one of our visits east. I haven't sung it in a while. I imagine you have forgotten it. It is not how I usually wake you. When you were little I used to wake you by singing *modeh ani.* I have not done that in a while either. This is a good reminder. I must start to sing *modeh ani* again. There's something about Hebrew words setting the tone for the day. "*Modeh ani lefanecha.*" Thank You, God, for restoring my soul to me in compassion.

I remember watching Grandpa Hy, my mother's father, in his home office in Scarsdale, New York, praying before he went off to be a lawyer. He would drape himself in his prayer shawl, wrap himself in his phylacteries, and pray as if his life depended on it. He would not leave his house to enter the secular world before he addressed God.

My Grandma Dorothy, his wife, also gave me an interesting perspective on faith. I don't think she is a believer. But she was proud of her husband, of his faith, of her granddaughter and her faith. Years after my grandfather died, I entered rabbinical school. When I visited my Grandma Dorothy, I prayed in her apartment draped in my prayer shawl and wrapped in my phylacteries, as my Grandpa Hy had done. She said to me, "Don't *nudgy* [bother] God too much." She never took herself too seriously, and thought no one should take themselves too seriously either. An important lesson on this journey of faith.

Another important role model for me: my Grandpa Shleimela, my father's father. He was also a rabbi, an Orthodox rabbi, and to me, he seemed to possess a deep faith in God.

I can't quite explain it, but when I was with him, I felt in awe of his faith. He seemed so steadfast, so certain. I wondered how he could be so certain. How anyone could be so certain. I didn't feel there was a way I would ever attain such deep certainty regarding my faith.

When I was in college, I spoke to my Grandma Ruth, his wife, about this fear of mine. She told me not to worry. She assured me that one day I would come to a faith of my own. Though she did not use the words, "Go forth," or as a Hasidic commentator once said, "Go to yourself," this is precisely what she meant and she spoke with such confidence I believed her.

I wonder what experiences you will see when you look back on your life, what stories you will find that influenced your faith or lack of faith in God. How you will put it all together. Will you remember my telling you the midrash highlighting the holiness of conception, the midrash of how when a child is created, mother, father, and God are present in this act of creation?

I told you this when you were three or four. You listened without question. Then one day, out of the clear blue, you asked, "Mama, how did God get me inside your tummy? God couldn't do dat."

As I grew up, I wasn't sure I always believed in God. I questioned God often. Especially when Rafi was dying of cancer.

God, how come you gave my eleven-year-old brother cancer? Any God that does that I cannot believe in. I talked with my father about it. He said, he didn't believe it was God. He said, he believed there were forces outside God's control. I remember thinking, then why believe in God, if God is not able to be God, but I have come to understand the wisdom of my father's comment.

I hope you end up a believer. Not with the blind belief of a child, but with the less blind belief of an adult. I want you to feel you can question God, confront God, argue with God, as I did, as I do.

Abraham questioned God. When God was going to destroy the city of Sodom, Abraham confronted God. He took God to task, saying essentially, Shouldn't You, God, Judge of the entire world, judge justly? (Genesis 18:25).

Moses challenged God. After the Israelites built the golden calf, Moses begged God not to be angry with the people of Israel, whom God had delivered from Egypt. He pleaded with God to let go of anger, and not to punish the people (Exodus 32:11–12).

The Psalmist questioned God, asking God why God stays far away, why God hides Godself in difficult times (Psalms 10:1).

The Hasidic masters questioned God. A story is told about Rabbi Levi Yitzchak of Berditchev and a tailor who had an argument with God on Yom Kippur. Levi Yitzchak asked the tailor what this argument was about. Said the tailor, "I declared to God: You wish me to repent of my sins, but I have committed only minor offenses … But [You], O God, [have] committed grievous sins: [You have] taken away babies from their mothers, and mothers from their babies. Let us be quits: [may You] forgive me, and I will forgive [You]." Rabbi Levi Yitzchak responded: "Why did you let God off so easily? You might have forced [God] to redeem all of Israel." (Newman, *The Hasidic Anthology*, 57). [Brackets indicate where I have converted old English to colloquial English.]

Gabriel, question God. Ask God: Why the good suffer? Why the Holocaust? Why a child is born who will not live into adulthood? Why parents abuse their children? Ask God your questions. Ask God for help understanding. To grapple with God is to believe. To grapple with God is to be in relationship with God.

Relationships work two ways. We ask God questions. God asks us questions.

Questions we should try to answer.

As God walked through the Garden of Eden, God asked Adam and Eve, "*Ayecha*?" "Where are you?" (Genesis 3:9). "Where are you?" God asks us, God asks you. Where are you in your relationship with God? With Judaism? Where are you in your relationship with yourself?

Another question God calls upon us to answer, the question God called out to Cain after he killed his brother Abel. "Where is Abel, your brother?" (Genesis 4:9). God asks us, God asks you. Where are your friends? Your neighbors? Where is your family? Your community? Do you understand, in this world of me-me-me, you are responsible not only for yourself, but for others?

Yet another two questions God calls upon us to answer: the questions put to Hagar when she ran away from Sarah. An angel of God found Hagar in the wilderness, and asked her from where she came and to where she was going (Genesis 16:8).

God asks each of us these questions. God challenges each of us to find our way. God asks you these questions. Answer them and find your way.

Be careful in judgment. If I was too quick to judge another person's failings or mistakes, my father would say to me, "Don't judge others. Don't hold yourself above others. You never know how you would act in a similar situation."

Instead of translating the text in Leviticus, "You should love your neighbor as yourself," Martin Buber said translate it as, "You should love your neighbor, he or she is a person like you." That was my father's understanding. When we remember others are like us, we are less likely to judge.

I hope your father and I have instilled within you this quality. I have to admit, I'm not always so good at modeling it. Your father is better at this than I am. He is more able to find the good in people. So far, you take after him in this way, and I am grateful.

Both of your hearts are absent of envy, and more generous than mine. "Good job. Great job. Didn't Sam do a great job, Mama?" you will say even if Sam is doing a better job than you are. Maybe you are not yet aware enough. Or, your self-esteem is high enough. Whatever the reason, I sense that you look for the good in people and I continue to learn from you.

From our tradition, I think, though I have no idea where, nor do I have a citation for this text:

When the angels learn that God intends to create human beings using the divine image, they are threatened. They believe that this creative act will result in their losing political clout with God. So they decide to hide the divine image. All kinds of suggestions are proposed. Each one of them is flawed. Then the winning suggestion is made. "Hide the divine image inside the human being. No one will look for it there."

But that is not true for you, Gabriel. You know where to look.

Responsibility. If it's true that every rabbi has only one sermon he or she delivers over and over again, my father's sermon is: responsibility. From his bar mitzvah speech to my brother, your Uncle Ari. "You are what you do. You are responsible for what you do. Do not blame the flame."

My mother also taught us to take responsibility for our actions. When we came to her to complain, "Sarina took my underwear," "Ari took my markers," "Rafi took my bubble gum," "Elana ate my candy," my mother would always say, "This is between you." Or, "Work it out among yourselves."

Since you have no siblings, this lesson does not occur all that often, though I use it when you have friends over. As to taking responsibility, we've been working on that since you were a toddler. Thanks to your Montessori education, you always take responsibility for your toys. What you take out, you put away. You help us set the table, clear the table, vacuum. You are responsible.

We are responsible to pursue justice. (Deuteronomy 16:20). So important is this responsibility, the word justice is repeated twice. On Martin Luther King Day, about a month before you turned five, we watched a video of his "I Have a Dream" speech, a tradition we started when you were two or three.

When the video clip of Dr. King ended, we talked about how it's wrong to treat people differently just because they have different colored skin. We talked about how Dr. King stood up for justice in the world, how powerful he was, how lots of people listened to him, how it's too bad that he was killed, because he could have done much more for our society had he lived. We also talked about Rosa Parks, whom you learned about in school, and her actions to help desegregate the busses in Alabama.

I told you how you, too, could stand up for justice. That when you grew up you could be a speaker for justice "Try it," I suggested. And you did. You stood up on the chair and started delivering a speech in a loud and powerful voice, about how brown people should not sit at the back of the bus and about how white people should treat brown people fairly. I cried as I listened to such deep feeling emerge from your little body.

Tzedekah, righteousness, comes from the word *tzedek*, justice. *Tzedekah* has come to stand for giving charity. We talk about how we show righteousness by giving money to those in need. I tell you how I write out checks to organizations that help people, The American Jewish World Service, Alyn Hospital in Israel, which helps physically disabled children. And other charities as well. Disaster relief funds for those suffering from earthquakes, tsunamis. And you understand. You understand that when your *tzedakah* box is full, we will decide together where we will send the money. Though we haven't put *tzedekah* in for a while now. We must start putting *tzedekah* in again. The box must not sit there as an adornment. You see, I fall short of doing all I want to do with you. I start something, and then I don't always carry it through. Most of the time I do, but not always. I must get better at that.

We often talk about forgiveness. We talk about how we're responsible to say we're sorry when we've done something wrong. I model this. I have had many opportunities to do so. I have committed many mistakes. Sometimes I head down to the basement to put in a load of laundry, tell you I will be up in a minute, and return five minutes later to find you in tears. You yell at me. "Mama, you promised you'd be right back. It's taken you a long time." "You're right," I say. "It's my fault. I blew it. I moved slower than I thought. I'm sorry. Please forgive me."

So far, you have always forgiven me when I ask, for whatever it is that I need to be forgiven. For that I'm grateful. And I tell you. "It feels good to be forgiven," I say. "It also feels good to forgive. Like when you say you're sorry to me, how I love to forgive you. That's what's cool about being human, we can forgive each other, and by forgiving each other we get closer."

I know it's sometimes hard to ask for forgiveness. I know it's sometimes hard to forgive. But that's what it means to be human. And being human isn't always easy. Judaism understands that. Judaism understands that as human beings we struggle. The philosopher Franz Rosenzweig once said, "I wish I were a symphony by Beethoven, or something else that has been completely written. What hurts is the process of being written."

The process of being written is a struggle. I've had many struggles. One we share: Being a perfectionist. I wanted to be perfect. If not perfect then almost perfect. And well into my adult life. If I didn't read Torah perfectly, I got angry with myself. If I didn't deliver the perfect sermon, I did not deserve to be a rabbi.

You, too, have this inclination. If you don't get something right the first time, you get angry with yourself. If you're reading a book, you close the book and decide it's no longer reading time. If you're coloring, you rip up what you have just created.

You're getting better with time. For that I am glad. It's hard to watch you struggle with something I struggled with for so long. My hope is that you will learn quicker than I did.

I've learned as I've grown that there is no way I can be perfect and I find comfort in the fact that Judaism recognizes this. On Rosh Hashanah and on Yom Kippur, we learn that Judaism is not about being perfect, but about being human.

Being human means making mistakes. Being human means taking responsibility for our mistakes, learning how to correct them, and growing from the experience.

The goal in Judaism is not perfection. The goal is wholeness. And wholeness is the opposite of perfection. To be whole means to be imperfect. Because when we are imperfect we are more whole. Who is more whole? A person with a broken heart, or a person whose heart has never been broken?

Gabriel, I thank God for bringing you into my life. My life is richer and more meaningful because of your presence. I thank you for challenging me with your questions. For holding me to my word. For loving me with all my imperfections.

I hope you continue to survive my parenting. My not always following through. The fact that I'm hard on you at times. Not too hard. But I do expect a lot from you. Not because you are an only child. But because you are you. You should know that however hard I am on you I'm twice as hard on myself.

I hope we have many more years together. I hope I have the opportunity to write you a few more forever letters. But when I'm no longer around, you will at least have this letter to remind you how much you are loved, and how much love you have to give.

The final words of my father's forever letter to me, Sarina, Ari, and Rafi resonate in my mind and heart, so much so that I use his words to end my letter to you.

"Say *kaddish* after me when I die, for me, for you, for Israel, for God, for you. I have always thanked God for you. May God continue to watch over you.

Always and always."

Love,
Mom

Appendix C: Quick Notes for Writing Your Forever Letter

In this appendix, I have included the sentence completions and the questions from chapter 8 to enable you to have easy access to these prompts as you begin to generate material for your forever letter.

Sentence Completions

1. The values I believe in are...

2. The values I believe in and find hard to live are...

3. Here's what I learned from my parents...

4. Here's what I wish I had learned from my parents...

5. Here's what I learned from my grandparents, grandchildren, sister(s), brother(s), children, teachers, students, aunts, uncles, mentors, friends (choose one for each three-minute write)...

6. The most important people in my life are/were...

7. The stories that have guided me in my life are...

8. The most meaningful lessons I have learned have been...

9. My strengths as a person are...

10. My strengths as a daughter (son), sister (brother), partner (spouse), wife (husband), mother (father), grandmother (grandfather), other family member or friend are...

11. My weaknesses as a person are...

12. My weaknesses as a daughter (son), sister (brother), partner (spouse), wife (husband), mother (father), grandmother (grandfather), other family member or friend are...

13. The most powerful gift(s) I have to offer is (are)...

14. The most powerful gift(s) I have received is (has been)...

15. My personal challenges and struggles have been...

16. I've lived up to my ideals by...

17. I've fallen short of my ideals by...

18. What I most want to tell the people I love about me...

19. What I most want to tell the people I love about them...

20. I love you because...

21. These are your strengths...

22. Here is what you have taught me...

23. My hopes for you are...

24. As I review my life, I regret...

25. As I review my life, I'm grateful for...

26. Please forgive me for...

27. I forgive myself for...

28. I'm trying to forgive myself for...

29. I can't forgive myself for...

30. I forgive you for...[112]

31. What I most want to be remembered for...

32. My blessings for you are...

33. May you...

QUESTIONS

1. Describe a time in your life when an important value was formed. Why is this value so important to you?

2. What is the most precious gift you have ever received? Was it an actual gift? Was it words? Was it an experience you shared with someone you love(d)? Why was this gift so meaningful?

3. What are your top ten values? Are you living these values? Why? Why not?

4. What organizations do you belong to? Why?

5. What organizations do you contribute to? Why?

6. Do the organizations you belong to and contribute to match your values?

---

112 This one entry in this list is from Jack Riemer and Nathaniel Stampfer, *So That Your Values Live On—Ethical Wills and How to Prepare Them* (Woodstock, VT: Jewish Lights Publishing, 2003), 231.

7. What values do you want to share with the person(s) you're writing to?

8. Who are (were) the ten most important people in your life? Why?

9. What are the ten most important causes in your life? Why?

10. What are the ten most important objects in your life? What does each represent? Did you acquire these objects on your own or were they given to you? By whom?

11. What words have helped you move forward in your life? What words have held you back? Who delivered these words?

12. What messages have your parents, children, grandparents, grandchildren, siblings, teachers, students, mentors, friends left you with?

13. What do you most want the recipient of your words to understand about you? How would knowing these things about you help your relationship?

14. Can you trace any of your values back to a certain moment in time? Do you recall when any of your values originated? Who helped to instill these values? How? Why?

15. If you died tomorrow, what would the people closest to you say about you?

16. In the novel *Demian: The Story of Emil Sinclair's Youth*, Hermann Hesse wrote: "If you hate a person, you hate something in him that is part of yourself. What isn't part of ourselves doesn't disturb us." [113] What irritates you about the person(s) you're writing to? Make a list. When you're done creating that list, circle those

---

113   Hesse, *Demian*, 97.

irritations that bother you about yourself. Ask yourself if there's any way you can be kinder toward and less judgmental of yourself. Can you carry this kindness over to others?

17. Consider these words from the philosopher, poet, and political activist Abraham Joshua Heschel: "The problem we face, the problem I as a father face, is why my child should revere me. Unless my child will sense in my personal existence acts and attitudes that evoke reverence—the ability to delay satisfactions, to overcome prejudices, to sense the holy, to strive for the noble—why should she revere me?" [114] Then answer the question: What about me deserves the reverence of my child, grandchild, parent, grandparent, niece, nephew, uncle, aunt, teacher, student, friend?

---

114   Abraham Joshua Heschel, *The Insecurity of Freedom* (New York: Farrar, Straus and Giroux, 1966), 39–40.

GRATITUDES

To my mother and father, Ann and Joel Zaiman, thank you for your love, compassion, support, and guidance over the years, and for your encouragement to take a year off to write this book. Dad, thanks for your initial suggestions when I struggled with how to contemplate such a large project. Mom, thanks for your presence and patience that first week in January 2012, when I went on a personal retreat to begin the writing of this book, and I called you, afraid that I wasn't up to the task, and you assured me that I was. You both continued to reassure me as I wrote and rewrote over a period of five years, and you continue to reassure me to this day.

To my sister, Sarina Zaiman Davis, and to my brother, Ari Zaiman, thank you for loving me, for putting up with me, and for believing in me all these years. Sarina, thank you for reading this book multiple times, for your honest and thoughtful feedback, and your humorous commentary. You can always make me laugh. To my brother, Rafi Zaiman, thank you for loving me while you were here on this earth. You're still so much a part of our family and you continue to occupy a large lot in the real estate of our hearts.

To my mother-in-law, Carol Remz, thank you for being an avid supporter of mine from our first meeting, and an enthusiastic promoter of this book—even before my words hit the page. Thank you for accompanying me to some workshops, both in and out of state, for your feedback, love, support, help at all stages along the way, and for meditating your way into the forever letter as a concept. To my father-in-law, Larry Sagen, thank you for your extensive and thoughtful comments on this book, and for your guidance, love, and support from your marketing expertise on the initial book proposal to your continued marketing and publicity support as I prepared to launch this book. I know I wrote about giving and gratitude in chapter 4, but I have a whole new take on them now. I am so grateful for your giving unconditionaly, without even being asked. I feel so blessed with you by my side.

To my husband, Seth Rosenbloom, thank you for confidence, your love, compassion, encouragement, and support. For hearing me when I said I needed to take a year off to get started on this book. For giving me time to write. For helping me to protect my writing time. For making me delicious meals. For believing in me when I had trouble believing in myself. For listening to me perseverate. For helping me live into myself.

To my son, Gabriel Zaiman Rosenbloom, who delighted in seeing my progress and who was constantly amazed by the number of drafts I had to write to get it just right. Even as I write this, I realize that I can never get this book into perfect condition, but that I must let it go, as it is good enough, and that is good enough for me. Thank you for honoring my writing time and for being proud of me.

To a master teacher, to my mentor, and friend, Priscilla Long, author of *The Writer's Portable Mentor*, who edited two versions of this manuscript, and without whom I would never have developed the skills I needed to write this book, nor would I have had the courage to write it. Your generosity of spirit knows no bounds. If your compassion and kindness could be bottled and sprayed throughout the world, the world would be a better place.

To my friend, Ruth Etzioni, who tended to this book and to me with care, compassion, and love. Thank you for hours of your time and for your extensive and insightful edits. I had a gut sense it was your help that I needed to take this book to the next level. I was right. I could not have done it without you. I am beyond grateful.

To my editor, Beth Lieberman, whose keen eye, wisdom, vision, patience, and guidance equipped and empowered me to reenter this book and to view it anew. I am grateful. I remain in awe of your editing insights and look forward to our continued connection and ongoing friendship.

To my friend and teacher Jana Harris, who upon hearing about this book, offered in her big-heart way, to read it. Jana, thank you. Your edits helped me bring my writing closer to publication.

To Pat Andrews, who copyedited this manuscript: I can't even count how many times—once when I first thought it was done, and then again when it was done for the second, third, and fourth time, maybe even fifth and sixth? Pat, you were beyond a copyeditor, offering astute editorial guidance and advice that helped me clarify my writing and tighten this book. Beyond your copyediting skills, your support, reassurance, and hope throughout this process gave me strength. I am blessed to have found a new friend.

To my agent, Susanna Einstein, whose belief in this book appeared at just the right time. Gratitudes beyond gratitudes for finding this book a home.

Gratitudes to the entire Llewellyn team. To Angela Wix, Acquisitions Editor, for your excellent editorial suggestions, present-ness, generosity of time and spirit. To Laura Graves, Production Editor, and Andy Belmas, Copywriter, for tending to all the details to ready this manuscript for publication. To Ellen Lawson, Cover Designer, and to Bob Gaul, Production Designer, for your artistic sensibilities. To Kat Sanborn, Senior Publicist, for all you are doing to launch this book into the world. For Bobbi O'Connor and Mary Ruud, for dealing with the intricacies of book purchases and deliveries, and to all of you behind the scenes who enable the flow, thank you.

To the rabbinic colleagues who invited me to their communities to serve as scholar-in-residence and to the social service agencies, retirement homes, interfaith groups, financial planning agencies, law firms, conference planners, and individuals who invited me to speak, teach, and conduct day-long workshops, I am grateful for your support.

To those of you who attended my workshops, who trusted me with your stories, concerns, fears, joys, and letters, who suggested books for me to read and movies for me to see, who asked questions that took me deeper in to my material and myself, this book would not be without you.

To the early readers of this manuscript: Ann Zaiman, Joel Zaiman, Carol Remz, Sarina Zaiman Davis, Fredelle Spiegel, Linda Breneman, Andrea Lewis, Neil Mathison; and to the later readers of this manuscript: Joyce Greenberg, Seth Rosenbloom, Larry Sagen, blessings. I'm grateful to all of you for your time, critical reads, invaluable contributions, and written feedback, to which I returned again and again. Thanks, too, to the writers in Priscilla's Monday class who, over the years, offered feedback on different sections of this book.

Gratitudes to these magazines and journals that published my articles. Portions of this text were originally published by *Rayonot: A Journal of Ideas*, *JT News*, *Jo Lee Magazine*, and *Bar News* (Washington State Bar Association). Some portions of this text were originally published by Wise Publishing Group, 2013, 2014, 2015, and 2016. Thanks, also, to Rachel Cowan and Linda Thal, who quoted my work on ethical wills in their book, *Wise Aging* (Behrman House).

I am indebted to Israel Abrahams for his scholarly work, *Hebrew Ethical Wills*, and to Jack Riemer and Nathaniel Stampfer for *Ethical Wills: A Modern Jewish Treasury*; for it was with these volumes that I began my study of ethical wills. Thanks, too, to Barry K. Baines for his work on ethical wills. Special appreciation to The Seattle Public Library's Research Department, and to Melissa Flamson and Margaret Gaston from With Permission for researching citations and acquiring permissions. Special appreciation also to Rabbi David Roth at The Yeshiva University Library for locating the Hebrew ethical will of Mordechai Mottel Michelsohn, to Rabbi Dr. Moshe Shualy and to Mordechai Shualy for translating this document, to Rabbi Dr. Moshe Shualy for highlighting the critical feature of the Master Paradigm, and to Rabbi Moshe Schapiro for researching several Hebrew citations.

BIBLIOGRAPHY

Abrahams, Israel. *Hebrew Ethical Wills*. Philadelphia: The Jewish Publication Society, 2006.

Abrahams, Israel. *Hebrew Ethical Wills*. Translated from this volume by Rabbi Dr. Moshe Shualy (unpublished, 2014). Philadelphia: The Jewish Publication Society, 2006.

Angelou, Maya. *Letter to My Daughter*. New York: Random House, 2008.

Bailie, Gil. *Violence Unveiled: Humanity at the Crossroads*. New York: Crossroad, 1995.

Baines, Barry K. *Ethical Wills: Putting Your Values on Paper*. Cambridge, MA: Da Capo Press, 2006.

Baldwin, James. "My Dungeon Shook." In *Collected Essays*. Edited by Toni Morrison. New York: The Library of America, 1998: 291–295.

Becker, Ernest. *The Denial of Death*. New York: Free Press, 1997.

Bok, Sissela. *Lying: Moral Choice in Public and Private Life*. New York: Vintage Books, 1979.

Bombeck, Erma. *Motherhood: The Second Oldest Profession*. New York: McGraw-Hill, 1983.

Borysenko, Joan. *Minding the Body, Mending the Mind*. Reading, MA: Addison-Wesley, 1987.

Brown, Brené. *Daring Greatly: How the Courage to Be Vulnerable Transforms the Way We Live, Love, Parent, and Lead*. New York: Gotham Books, 2012.

Brown, Tricia Gates. "The Eighth Sacrament." *The University of Portland Magazine* 32, no. 1 (Spring 2013): 17–18.

Browne, Lewis. *The World's Great Scriptures*. London: MacMillian, 1946.

Buber, Martin. *I and Thou*. New York: First Scribner Classic/Collier Edition, 1987.

———. *Tales of the Hasidim: The Early Masters*. New York: Schocken Books, 1975.

Carlyle, Hadiyah Joan. *Torch in the Dark*. Bothell, WA: Book Publishers Network, 2012.

Carpenter, Liz. *Getting Better All the Time*. College Station, TX: Texas A&M University Press, 1993.

Chang, June. "Dear Granddaughter" in *Letter to My Grandchild* edited by Liv Ullmann. New York: Atlantic Monthly Press, 1998.

Choquette, Sonia. *Trust Your Vibes: Secret Tools for Six-Sensory Living*. Carlsbad, CA: Hay House, 2004. Kindle edition.

Clark, Dan. *Weathering the Storm*. New York: British American Publishing, 1990.

Couturie, Bill. *Last Letters Home: Voices of Americans from the Battlefields of Iraq*. United States: HBO Studios, 2005. Also, as book: New York: Life Books, 2004.

Dan, Joseph. "Wills, Ethical." In vol. 16 of *Encyclopaedia Judaica*. Jerusalem, Israel: Keter Publishing House, 1972.

Didion, Joan. "Why I Write" in *New York Times Book Review*, December 5, 1976.

Dillard, Annie. *The Writing Life*. New York: Harper & Row, 1989.

Edelman, Marian Wright. *The Measure of Our Success: A Letter to My Children and Yours*. New York: HarperPerennial, 1993.

Elbow, Peter. *Writing Without Teachers*. New York: Oxford University Press, 1973.

Forster, E. M. *Howards End*. New York: Alfred A. Knopf, 1921.

Foster, Rick, and Greg Hicks. *How We Choose to Be Happy: The 9 Choices of Extremely Happy People—Their Secrets, Their Stories*. New York: Perigee, 1999.

Fredrickson, Barbara. *Positivity*. New York: Crown, 2009.

Glückel of Hameln. *The Memoirs of Glückel of Hameln*. Translated by Marvin Lowenthal. New York: Schocken Books, 1977.

Goldberg, Natalie. *Writing Down the Bones*. Boston: Shambhala Publications, 1986.

Gordon, Arthur. *A Touch of Wonder*. Old Tappan, NJ: Fleming H. Revell, 1974.

Green, Arthur. *Ehyeh: A Kabbalah for Tomorrow*. Woodstock, VT: Jewish Lights Publishing, 2004.

Heschel, Abraham Joshua. *The Insecurity of Freedom*. New York: Farrar, Straus and Giroux, 1966.

Hesse, Hermann. *Demian: The Story of Emil Sinclair's Youth*. New York: Harper Perennial, Modern Classics 2009, originally published 1999.

Hughes, Langston. *The Collected Poems of Langston Hughes*. Edited by Arnold Rampersad and David Roessel. New York: Alfred A. Knopf, 2007.

Imam al-Nawawi. "Hadith 13". bible-quran.com/hadith-13-imam-nawawi-isla/.

Irving, Washington. In *Dictionary of Quotations*. Compiled by James Wood. London and New York: Frederick Warner & Co., 1899. Also Bartleby.com, 2012. www.bartleby.com/345/authors/258.html. Also attributed to Samuel Johnson in Daniel B. Quinby, editor. *Monthly Literary Miscellany, Vols. 6-7*. Quinby, Wood, & Russel, 1852.

Isaacson, Walter. "American Icon." *Time*. October 17, 2011.

Kabat-Zinn, Jon. *Full Catastrophe Living: Using the Wisdom of Your Body and Mind to Face Stress, Pain, and Illness*. New York: Delta Trade Paperbacks, 2009.

Kidd, Sue. "Don't Let It End This Way." *Guidepost Magazine*, November 2006, vol. 61, issue 9.

Kingsolver, Barbara. "Letter to a Daughter at Thirteen." In *Small Wonder*. New York: Perennial, 2003.

Klagsbrun, Francine. *Voices of Wisdom: Jewish Ideals and Ethics for Everyday Living*. Middle Village, NY: Jonathan David Publishers, 1986.

Klopsch, Louis. *Many Thoughts of Many Minds*. Teddington, UK: Echo Library, 2008.

Knapp, Caroline. *Drinking a Love Story*. New York: Delta Trade Paperbacks, 1996.

Kübler-Ross, Elisabeth. *Death: The Final Stage of Growth*. New York: Simon & Schuster, 1975.

Kurosawa, Akira. *Something Like an Autobiography*. New York: Vintage Books, 1983.

Lamott, Anne. *Bird by Bird: Some Instructions on Writing and Life*. New York: Anchor Books Doubleday, 1995.

Lawson, Dorie McCullough. *Posterity: Letters of Great Americans to Their Children*. New York: Doubleday, 2004.

Long, James A. *Expanding Horizons*. Pasadena, CA: Theosophical University Press, 1990.

Luskin, Fred. *Forgive for Good: A Proven Prescription for Health and Happiness*. New York: HarperSanFrancisco, 2002.

Lynch, Thomas. "Limning the Rites of Death." In *The Life of Meaning: Reflections on Faith, Doubt, and Repairing the World,* edited by Bob Abernethy and William Bole. New York: Seven Stories Press, 2008.

Markova, Dawna. "May we learn to open in love … " In *Prayers for Healing: 365 Blessings, Poems, & Meditations from Around the World*. Edited by Maggie Oman Shannon. Boston: Conari Press, 2000.

Martin, Gregory. *Stories for Boys*. Portland, OR: Hawthorne Books & Literary Arts, 2012.

Mayo Clinic News Network. "10 Tips for Better Health." Mayo Clinic News Network, May 4, 2011. www.businesswire.com/news /home/ 20110505006693/en/Mayo-Clinic-Health-Letter-2011 -Highlights-10.

Memorybridge. "Gladys Wilson and Naomi Feil." YouTube. Posted May 26, 2009. www.youtube.com/watch?v=CrZXz10FcVM.

Mendel, Menachem, of Kotzk. *Amud Ha'Emet: Teachings, Sayings, Discussions and Life of Our Teacher R. Menachem Mendel of Kotzk.* Collected and edited by Moshe Betzalel Alter. Tel Aviv, Israel: Pe'er Publishing, 5760 (1999–2000).

Michelsohn, Mordechai Mottel. "The Ethical Will of Mordechai Mottel Michelsohn." In *Sefer Beit Meshulem.* Edited by Rabbi Natan Natah Kronenberg, n.p., 1905.

Newman, Louis I. *The Hasidic Anthology: Tales and Teachings of the Hasidim.* Northvale, NJ: Jason Aronson, 1987.

Obama, Barack. "What I Want for You—and Every Child in America." *Parade Magazine,* January 18, 2009, 5.

Ozick, Cynthia. *Crafting Prose.* Edited by Don Richard Cox and Elizabeth Giddens. San Diego, CA: Harcourt Brace Jovanovich, 1991.

Palmer, Parker J. "The Clearness Committee: A Communal Approach to Discernment," at Center for Courage and Renewal website, www.couragerenewal.org.

———. *Let Your Life Speak: Listening for the Voice of Vocation.* San Francisco: Jossey-Bass, 2000.

Pausch, Randy. *The Last Lecture.* New York: Hyperion, 2008.

Pickford, Mary. "Why Not Try God?" *St. Petersburg Times,* sect. 2, January 25, 1936.

Picoult, Jodi. "An Open Letter to My Oldest Son, as He Leaves for College." In *Leaving Home: Short Pieces.* Newton Highlands, MA: LGLA/Kindle Single, 2011.

Platt, Norbet. "Norbert Platt Quote" at IZ Quotes. www.izquotes.com /quote/302453.

Reichl, Ruth. *Not Becoming My Mother and Other Things She Taught Me along the Way*. New York: Penguin, 2009.

Zhang, Yimou, and Yasuo Furuhata. *Riding Alone for Thousands of Miles*, DVD. United States: Sony Pictures Classics, 2005.

Riemer, Jack, and Nathaniel Stampfer. *Ethical Wills: A Modern Jewish Treasury*. New York: Schocken Books, 1983.

———. *So That Your Values Live On—Ethical Wills and How to Prepare Them*. Woodstock, VT: Jewish Lights, 2003.

Rilke, Rainer Maria. *Letters to a Young Poet*. Translated by Stephen Mitchell. New York: Random House, 1986.

Robinson, Marilynne. *Gilead*. New York: Farrar, Straus Giroux, 2004.

Rudavsky, Oren, and Manachem Daum. *Hiding and Seeking: Faith and Tolerance after the Holocaust*, DVD. San Francisco, CA: Independent Television Service, 2004.

Saroyan, William. *The Human Comedy*. New York: Dell, 1971.

Segal David. "Parent Trap." Interview with Rebecca Gee, episode 401, *This American Life*, Chicago Public Media. February 19, 2010, www.thisamericanlife.org/radio-archives/episode/401/parent-trap.

Selzer, Richard. *Mortal Lessons: Notes on the Art of Surgery.* New York: Harcourt Brace, 1996.

Shakespeare, William. *Hamlet*. In *The Oxford Shakespeare*. Edited by W. J. Craig. London: Oxford University Press, 1914.

Shulman, Y. David. *The Chambers of the Palace: Teachings of Rabbi Nachman of Bratslav*. Northvale, NJ: Jason Aronson, 1993.

Stanton, Elizabeth Cady. "Elizabeth Cady Stanton to Margaret L. Stanton, December 1, 1872." In *The Papers of Elizabeth Cady Stanton, 1814–1946,* Library of Congress. hdl.loc.gov/loc.mss/ eadmss.ms998020.

Stovall, Jim. *The Ultimate Gift.* Colorado Springs, CO: David C. Cook, 2007.

Taylor, Susan L. "In The Spirit." In Essence, October 1992, 55.

Tanakh: The Holy Scriptures, The New JPS Translation According to the Traditional Hebrew Text. Philadelphia: The Jewish Publication Society, 1988.

Telushkin, Joseph. *The Book of Jewish Values: A Day-by-Day Guide to Ethical Living.* New York: Bell Tower, 2000.

Teresa of Avila. *The Collected Works of St. Teresa of Avila*, vol. 2. Translated by Keiran Kavanaugh and Otilio Rodriguez. Washington, DC: ICS Publications, 1980.

Truitt, Anne. *Daybook: The Journal of an Artist.* New York: Penguin Books, 1984.

Valinsky, Jordan. "Study: It's Easier to Tell the Truth over Text So Why Bother Speaking Anymore?" Yahoo! news, December 23, 2013. www.news.yahoo.com/study-easier-tell-truth-over-text-why -bother-145506847.html.

Viorst, Judith. *Necessary Losses: The Loves, Illusions, Dependencies and Impossible Expectations That All of Us Have to Give Up In Order to Grow.* New York: Fawcett Gold Medal, 1987.

Vonnegut, Kurt. *A Man Without a Country.* New York: Seven Stories Press, 2005.

Ward, Chip. "A Letter of Apology to My Granddaughter." *Tom's Dispatch* (blog). March 27, 2012, www.tomdispatch.com/post/175521/.

Whiting, Roger. *Religions for Today*. London: Stanley Thornes, 1991.

Williams, William Carlos. "To William, September 25, 1942." In *The Selected Letters of William Carlos Williams*. Edited by John C. Thirwall. New York: McDowell, Obolensky, 1957.

Wiman, Christian. "Mortify Our Wolves." In *The American Scholar*, Autumn 2012, 59–71.

Wood, Nancy C. "Hold on to what is good." In *Many Winters: Poetry and Prose of the Pueblos*. Garden City, NY: Doubleday, 1974.

Wordsworth, William. Letter dated April 29, 1812. In *The Letters of William and Dorothy Wordsworth VIII: A Supplement of New Letters*. Edited by Alan G. Hill. Oxford, UK: Clarendon Press, 1993.

Wouk, Herman. *The Caine Mutiny*. Garden City, NY: Doubleday, 1951.